THE GOSPEL
AND
THE GAY

KENNETH O. GANGEL

THE GOSPEL
AND
THE GAY

Thomas Nelson Inc., Publishers
Nashville   New York

Unless otherwise indicated, all Scripture quotations are from the King James Version of the Bible.

Verses marked NASB are from the New American Standard Bible, © The Lockman Foundation 1960, 1962, 1963, 1968, 1971, 1972, 1973, 1975, and are used by permission.

Verses marked NIV are from the New International Version, New Testament, copyright © 1973 by the New York Bible Society International.

Verses marked RSV are from the Revised Standard Version of the Bible, copyrighted 1946, 1952, © 1971, 1973.

Verses marked TLB are taken from *The Living Bible* (Wheaton, Illinois: Tyndale House Publishers, 1971) and are used by permission.

Excerpts from *Homosexuality and the Western Christian Tradition* by Derrick Sherwin Bailey, © 1955 by Longmans and 1975 by Archon Books, are used by permission of the Longman Group Ltd. and Archon Books.

Library of Congress Cataloging in Publication Data

Gangel, Kenneth O
  The Gospel and the gay.

  Bibliography: p. 198
  1. Homosexuality and Christianity. I. Title.
BR115.H6G36   261.8'34'157   78-10378
ISBN 0-8407-5658-5

ACKNOWLEDGMENTS

The author is deeply grateful to a number of people without whose cooperation this manuscript could not have been prepared.

To the Board of Trustees of Miami Christian College for granting time for research, writing, and other scholarly activities.

To Burl A. DeLong for the opportunity to "tap in" to much of the research that he did in the preparation of his master's degree thesis at Dallas Theological Seminary.

To Chaplain David J. Pipping of the Apalachee Correctional Institute for arranging the interview testimony.

To Ed Dolansky, president of National Airlines, whose contribution to Miami Christian College during the struggle on the gay referendum in Dade County, Florida, made it possible for the college to print and circulate thousands of copies of "The Gospel and the Gay" in brochure form.

And to my faithful and competent secretary, Marjorie Wells, for laboring long and lovingly over a manuscript whose content she did not find particularly tasteful, but whose value she never doubted.

CONTENTS

FOREWORD

Not very long ago it would have been considered grossly impolite, if not downright indecent, to discuss homosexuality in a church service, despite the references to it in Scripture. But as James Russell Lowell writes, "New occasions teach new duties." So with the ever-increasing public advocacy of the gay life-style as a morally acceptable alternative to heterosexuality, it becomes the duty of the Christian ethicist and educator to examine this matter in depth from a Biblical perspective.

This is precisely what Dr. Kenneth Gangel does. Disclaiming the role of psychologist or sociologist, he focuses attention on the relevant insights and directives which can be drawn from a careful study of God's Word. At the same time he seeks to show how—with compassion and understanding—the church can minister redemptively to a segment of the human family that is treated as a rule with disdain and abhorrence.

The Gospel and the Gay will therefore prove of great help to evangelicals as they face one of today's—and no doubt tomorrow's—most urgent social issues.

Vernon C. Grounds
President
Conservative Baptist
Theological Seminary
Denver, Colorado

INTRODUCTION

On New Year's Day in 1965 a costume ball changed San Francisco as much as the earthquake and fire of 1906. At the same time, it changed a nation's attitude toward an understanding of the homosexual issue.

On that day a group of liberal Protestant ministers and their wives turned up at a homosexual dance in the hope that their presence would discourage mass arrests among the gay community they were defending. Police, having failed to persuade the operator of California Hall to cancel the rental agreement, lined up squad cars outside and photographed each of the six hundred guests as they arrived. Six arrests resulted since homosexual acts between consenting adults were still illegal at the time in California.

The next day San Francisco clergy called a news conference to denounce the police, and the nation's most concentrated homosexual community came out of the closet. Since that day, the financial and political clout of gays in San Francisco has been almost beyond belief. Gay advocate Richard Hongisto was elected sheriff and Mayor George Goscone appointed homosexuals to city commissions. Voters in a heavily gay district recently elected a homosexual,

Harvey Milk, to the city's board of supervisors. According to Robert Strand, a reporter for United Press International, "one out of six or seven adult San Franciscans is homosexual: from 70,000 to 150,000."[1]

In the same city (perhaps our own modern day Sodom), Tom Ammiano, a gay teacher, claims that one-third of the public school teachers and administrators are homosexual. Last May the school board voted 7-0 to revise the family life curriculum to eliminate negative references to gays.

Five years later, in June of 1970, Rev. Tom Maurer of San Francisco, president of the Society for Individual Rights, offered the press some statistics about the number of homosexuals in the United States. The occasion was an announcement by Father Robert L. Minton (a priest at St. Stevens Roman Catholic Church in Minneapolis) that members of FREE (Fight Repression of Erotic Expression), a homosexual group composed largely of University of Minnesota students, would be welcome at St. Stevens. Maurer (a Protestant minister) indicated that homosexuals comprise the second largest minority group in society (next to blacks), numbering from fifteen to twenty million people. Maurer claimed that employment discrimination was the largest single problem faced by the gay community.[2]

And in the spring of 1977 in Miami, where these words are being penned, activism by local homosexuals culminated in a so-called "Gay Rights Ordinance" passed by the metropolitan Dade County Commission. The six to three vote, which determined that there could be no discrimination in Dade

[1]*Fort Lauderdale News,* 4 December 1977, p. 18C.
[2]EP News Release, 6 June 1970.

County employment because of sexual preference, had the effect of forcing all employers (non-Christian or Christian, public or private) in the county to hire homosexuals if they otherwise met the qualifications of the job. The ordinance also required property owners to rent or sell domiciles to gays.

Singer Anita Bryant and Coral Gables City Commissioner Bob Brake launched Save Our Children, an interfaith organization created to help defeat the ordinance in a June referendum. The referendum was called after more than sixty thousand names were presented on petitions to the metro commission—a collection of signatures believed to be the most ever collected in such a short time in Dade County history. And the total represented fifty thousand more signatures than were needed to force a referendum.

The vote was the first referendum on the rights of homosexuals in any major U.S. city. Almost all of us in Dade County, including the political analysts, expected a close vote, but the antidiscrimination ordinance was repealed by a margin of more than two to one. There was an unusually large turn-out for a referendum (45 percent) and the ordinance was repealed by a 69 to 31 percent margin. *The Miami Herald,* which had urged repeal of the ordinance in a last-minute editorial, later described the whole referendum as a "climate of hysteria more appropriate to the 17th Century than the 20th."[3]

Although *Newsweek* magazine called the election a stunning setback for gay activists in their battle to extend civil-rights legislation,[4] gays everywhere appeared to take the defeat in Dade County in the best possible light. They expressed anger, but argued that

[3]"A 'No' To The Gays," *Newsweek,* 20 June 1977, p. 27.
[4]Ibid.

the national publicity of the Miami referendum might be the catalyst for uniting the gay community on a nation-wide basis. *Newsweek* maintained that gays had some hard work to do before the country was ready to accept homosexuality as an acceptable alternative life-style.

> Until now, they clearly interpreted recent gains in gay rights as a sign that the public at large no longer objected vehemently to homosexuality. And they clearly judged that the voters would not pay serious attention to Bryant's emotional fundamentalism. The Miami vote proved otherwise. In any coming national campaign, gay-rights leaders will have to mount a delicate and difficult re-education campaign if they expect to achieve any further measure of acceptance.[5]

Oddly enough, that is precisely the position of this book, only with respect to evangelical Christians. In the heat of the Save Our Children campaign (and I give the fullest credit to Anita Bryant for courage and conviction in the face of much abuse and personal sacrifice), Christians also failed to carry out any program of biblical education regarding homosexuality.

Instead the issues raised were perversion, molestation of children, communism, and the morality of society. Of course all of these matters were—and are—important. To the thinking evangelical, however, the ultimate issue is whether or not the Bible has anything to say on the subject, and if so, whether or not one wishes to take seriously whatever it is the Bible says.

So the purposes of this volume should be very clear at the outset. *It is designed to explore both the*

[5]Ibid.

biblical position on homosexuality and how that biblical position can be implemented in both church and society. It is not written to provide all of the psychological and sociological data relating to the vast complex of problems that homosexuality presents in this last quarter of the twentieth century. Nor is it aimed at raising concomitant political issues.

Quite obviously, it will be necessary to separate political issues from theological issues if the latter are to be intelligently discussed. It is my position, for example, that the Dade County ordinance and others like it really have very little to do with civil rights. But a secular press cannot grasp the significance of what it means to live in accordance with the dictates of Scripture. On June 10, 1977, *The Arizona Daily Star* published its editorial view on the Dade County election.

* Converting the ignorant and the innocent to anti-social behavior—such as child pornography—is decadence. Homosexuality as a lifestyle is not. Homosexual individuals offer as much individual variety of personality as any class of people.[6]

It is to test such a viewpoint against the litmus of divine revelation that this book has been written.

K.O.G.

Miami Christian College
Miami, Florida
Spring, 1978

[6]*The Arizona Daily Star,* 10 June 1977, p. 14.

THE GOSPEL
AND
THE GAY

CHAPTER 1

WHAT'S ALL
THE FUSS ABOUT?

On the night of June 28, 1969, New York police raided The Stonewall Inn, a Greenwich Village bar frequented by homosexuals. Homosexuals fought back and the rioting continued for two days. When it was all over, homosexuals were no longer "homosexual"—they were "gay." The term had been a code word prior to that night but now it was a "politicized euphemism" according to San Francisco State University anthropologist Robin Wells.

The principal difference, I suppose, was the reference to a life-style rather than just sexual preference or practice. The word "gay" is now like the word "black"—a note of pride in a movement. No doubt proponents of homosexuality prefer the term to "sodomites," "queers," "fairies," "pansies," "fruits," "faggots," and other words used to denounce the movement and its proponents. We'll talk later about whether "gay" really means "happy" in the traditional sense.

Psychologically, the movement has advanced rapidly in recent years. Rather than viewing himself as strictly abnormal as he formerly did, the

---

[1]*The Miami Herald,* 29 May 1977, Sec. G–E.

homosexual is moving toward self-acceptance. Indeed, the concept is in actuality a motto: "Self acceptance is the first step to happiness."[2]

The new tolerance is a little more difficult to come by on the streets. Traditionally, law enforcement officials have reserved a special contempt for deviants, although police aggressiveness toward homosexuals has been curbed by recent court decisions protecting their rights to socialize in private and also by the new assertiveness of homophile organizations operating in some fifty U.S. cities.[3]

In former days, gays attempted to press their case in society by the marches of masculine appearing women and effeminate men forcing the issue in bars and other public places. Today the National Gay Task Force epitomizes the new approach. Formed in 1973, it now represents more than twelve hundred nation-wide organizations, all geared to using legislation as a means to change society's values.

Basic Definitions

Perhaps it is best to begin by defining terms. When reading literature on the subject of homosexuality, one invariably runs into words like "gay," "straight," "effeminate," "lesbian," along with the more familiar "homosexual" and "heterosexual." The July/August 1973 issue of *Trends* magazine (released by the United Presbyterian Church) discussed the matter of homosexuality suggesting that the church accept it as a variant life-style since homosexual relationships are neither unnatural, sinful, nor

[2]"Gays on the March," *Time*, 8 September 1975, p. 32.
[3]"Policing the Third Sex," *Newsweek*, 27 October 1969, p. 76.

sick. Obviously, that denomination's program agency was hardly negative on "gayism" so its definitions probably represent a fair description of the terms listed above:

» Homosexual: Having a preference for intimate relationships with persons of the same sex.

Heterosexual: Having a preference for intimate relationships with persons of the opposite sex.

Gay: Being free from shame, guilt, misgivings, or regret over being homosexual.

Straight: Not deviating from the general or the prescribed pattern.[4]

The term "lesbianism" designates female homosexuality. The term "effeminate" is defined by Webster's *New Collegiate Dictionary* (1973 edition) as "having feminine qualities (as weakness or softness) inappropriate to a man: not manly in appearance or manner." It is *extremely important* to note that an effeminate person is not necessarily homosexual, though frequently the society tends to make that connection.

One can get even more specific in definitions as Charles Young did in an article in *His* magazine.

» Three additional terms may be noted in the literature on homosexuality. The term *overt* homosexual refers to the person participating in homosexual acts. The term *latent* homosexual refers to the person who has homosexual impulses but does not engage in homosexual behavior. *Pseudohomosexuality*, according to Ovesey, indicates a condition in which the person con-

[4]*Trends* (Program Agency of the United Presbyterian Church) (July/August 1973): 6.

vinces himself that he is homosexual because he has failed in some vocation or social task which is supposed to fulfill certain masculine requirements of our society.[5]

One other term might be mentioned—"homophobia"—the fear of homosexuals or fear that one might be homosexual. Particularly when homosexuality is featured in the media, it is common for many young people and adults who may have some of the symptoms commonly associated with homosexuality to fear that any serious friendship with members of the same sex may indicate a latent homosexuality. Letha Scanzoni speaks of the dangers of this reaction:

> The homophobic person is so revolted by the notion that persons of the same sex might relate to one another sexually, that he constantly seeks to reassure himself that no such tendencies exist in himself or in his children. At the same time, he is suspicious of any behavior that bears the remotest resemblance to his personal concepts of homosexuality, and he is ready to apply the label "perversion" to anything and everything from nonconformity to gender-role stereotypes to a deep friendship between two men or two women.[6]

Development of the Gay Movement

Dade County may have been the 1977 focal point, but the issue of homosexuality is hardly confined to

[5]"Homosexuality and the Campus," *HIS* (February 1966): 14.

[6]"On Friendship and Homosexuality," *Christianity Today* (27 September 1974): 11.

Miami. The Miami referendum was crucial because, at the time, twenty-five congressmen were pushing U.S. House of Representatives Bill 2998, which would impose on the entire nation the same kind of provisions enacted in the Miami ordinance. Indeed, the congressional bill goes even further, requiring all public schools to consider the hiring of homosexuals as teachers on the same basis as other applicants and the military to accept gays in its ranks.

Hardly new, homosexuality has existed since ancient times in a multitude of societies. On occasion it has actually been condoned in some societies for a segment of the population. According to Elizabeth Ogg, one can find examples of homosexuality ranging from the cultured Greeks to primitive tribes, such as the Aranda of Australia and the Kesaki of New Guinea.[7] Meanwhile, the Judeo-Christian heritage has maintained the rigid position that homosexuality is sexual perversion, and in most societies influenced by this heritage, homosexuality has actually been labeled an illegal practice.

The door was really opened when Alfred Kinsey exploded a 1948 bombshell on American society called *Sexual Behavior in the Human Male.* Thinking in the last three decades has gradually moved toward agreement with Kinsey's position that homosexual experiences are not as isolated as people once believed.[8]

Almost ten years after Kinsey's book, a new thrust in the homosexual movement was unleashed in the form of a report from the British Wolfenden Committee. That report, issued in 1957, recommended that

[7]*Homosexuality in our Society* (n.p.: Public Affairs Commission, 1975), p. 2.

[8]*Sexual Behavior in the Human Male* (Philadelphia: W. B. Saunders Co., 1948), pp. 616–17.

homosexual acts in private between consenting adults no longer be classified as illegal. Then the 1960s brought civil rights into focus and every minority group wanted to be liberated. All of a sudden, minorities were making themselves known everywhere, and by 1970 gays had begun to organize for social and political action.

Homosexuals and Politics

The current status of gay activism makes it impera tive that thinking Christians really understand the situation on the national scene. At the present time, thirty-two states still designate homosexual practices as crimes. But since 1961, eighteen states have eliminated sodomy laws that bar sexual acts between consenting adults. Many communities have approved ordinances prohibiting job, credit, and other discrimination on the basis of sexual preference, and I have already mentioned the congressional legislation that would add homosexuals to the list of groups that may not be discriminated against in public accommodations and employment.

Homosexuals are not only engaged in political activity on a general basis, but are actually running for and winning public offices. In 1974, thirty-two-year-old Elaine Noble became the first avowed lesbian to win state office in the United States when she was elected to the Massachusetts Legislature. She continues to have every intention of getting homosexual bills onto the floor of the legislature of that state.

In a magazine article, Jerrold K. Footlick and Susan Agrest report that activists also are making slow but steady progress on the legal front.

"There has been an enormous change in pub

lic attitudes over the past seven years," says National Gay Task Force Co-Director Gene O'Leary. "This has been reflected both in the laws and in private discriminatory policies." On balance, the prospect is that the activists will continue gradually to win more and more of the civil rights that have been denied to homosexuals in the past, and with these gains perhaps an increasing degree of public tolerance.[9]

There is certainly some connection between the political pressure for the Equal Rights Amendment (ERA) and the homosexual movement, though certainly the two are not always intrinsically connected. In fact it may be more correct to identify "homosexual lib" with certain leaders of the National Organization of Women. One of that organization's publications entitled "Struggle to End Sex Bias—Report on Sex Bias in the Public Schools" talks about "Lesbians and the Schools." The article is coauthored by Jean O'Leary, the co-executive director of the National Gay Task Force, who was also appointed by President Jimmy Carter to serve on the National Commission for the Observance of International Women's Year. In the article O'Leary makes the following recommendations:

> School counselors should be required to take courses in human sexuality in which a comprehensive and positive view of lesbianism is presented. Colleges which do not offer such courses ought to design and provide them. Lesbians, as well as heterosexual counselors, should be represented on the guidance staff.

In addition, the names and phone numbers of gay

[9] 'Gays and the Law," *Newsweek,* 25 October 1976, p. 103

counseling services should be made available to all students and school psychologists. Students should be given the opportunity, if they so desire, to contact these agencies.

No school counselor should ever refer a student to a psychotherapist for the purpose of changing her/his sexual preference from gay to straight. Such conditioning conveys to the student that her/his feelings of love are unworthy and unacceptable; it causes immeasurable conflict and ego damage, and can never be done in the name of mental health.[10]

But we didn't really understand how closely the homosexual issue was tied up with ERA until the Houston conference in late 1977. "Sexual pref erence," the feminist euphemism for lesbian rights was not on the original agenda for Houston, but the conference rules said that it had to be considered if ten or more state conventions asked for it. A thundering demand for a lesbian rights provision hit Houston from no fewer than thirty-six conventions! It passed.

An analysis of this lesbian rights provision by *Time* magazine said, "It calls for an end to discrimination on the basis of 'sex' and 'affectional preference' in child custody suits; in housing, employment, credit, public accommodations, government-funded projects in the military; and in state laws restricting 'private sexual behavior between consenting adults.' Let no one misunderstand that this provision is now related to the Equal Rights Amendment."[11]

Even the U.S. Supreme Court is now faced with

[10]Jean O'Leary and Ginny Vida, "Lesbians and the Schools," Homosexual Community Counseling Center, 921 Madison Avenue, New York.
[11]*Time*, 5 December 1977, p. 21.

the matter of ruling on legislation on homosexuality. As of September, 1977, the court is being asked to intervene in a dispute between the University of Missouri and a "gay-lib" student group. A lower federal court had already ordered the university to recognize gay liberation organizations on its Columbia and Kansas City campuses. Now the university has appealed to the Supreme Court saying that formal recognition would likely bring about on-campus violations of state sodomy laws. When the "gay-lib" group has had a chance to reply to the university's appeal, the Supreme Court will decide whether to hear the case or let the lower court decision stand.

Homosexuals and Ecclesiastical Action

Make no mistake about it, the church will be profoundly affected by this whole matter and particularly the so-called civil rights legislation. Gay activists clearly understand that support for legal and social change would be significantly advanced if the church approved of homosexuality. They may get their wish. It took 5,758 petitions to convince the hierarchy of the United Methodist church to refuse the General Church Study on Homosexuality, but the issue is by no means dead in the denomination.

There is also a great deal of pending ecclesiastical legislation regarding the gay movement. In the Roman Catholic church, a Detroit conference held in October of 1976 called for a more tolerant attitude toward birth control and homosexuality. But that position has already been dismissed by U.S. bishops who have reaffirmed the view that homosexual activity is morally wrong. This is in keeping with the Vatican Declaration on Sexual Ethics written in January, 1976: "Homosexual acts are intrinsically dis ordered and can in no way be approved of."[12]

Meanwhile, numerous denominations are facing votes at national meetings regarding their existing attitudes on homosexuality.

The United Presbyterian Church (UPC) appointed a task force to study the ordination of avowed practicing homosexuals, and the task force later recommended that the UPC ordain homosexuals as ministers. But in May of 1978, the General Assembly rejected this recommendation by a substantial margin. Time will tell if the issue is dead, however. The Southern Presbyterians are wavering, and the Episcopal church is in controversy with at least one bishop having already ordained an avowed lesbian to the ministry.

Protestantism's liberal voice, the National Council of Churches, endorsed the Miami pro-gay ordinance, a stand that was not surprising to anyone who has followed the NCC over recent decades.[13] Rev. Jerry R. Kirk, a United Presbyterian pastor in Cincinnati, has identified the crucial nature of denominational legislation regarding homosexuality:

> If those acts could now be redefined by the Church as not sin and not against the law of God and truth of Scripture, is there any other sin which could not also be so redefined? If that were to become the case, what basis for morality could the Church possibly proclaim? And if the roots of morality are pulled from the Biblical revelation, what is the meaning of salvation and what basis would the Church have for being the conscience

[12]"Replying To A Call For Action," *Time,* 16 May 1977, p. 75.

[13]G. Russell Evans, "What About the Homosexuals?" *The Presbyterian Journal* (30 November 1977): 7–8.

of and providing moral and spiritual leadership for our society? These questions must be answered by the people of God.[14]

The Christian and the Gay

Evangelical Christians need to be alert to the implications of this gay force in their communities, their churches, and their nation. But most of all they need to understand the underlying biblical and theological assumptions that have always made the church of Jesus Christ, though not always in an intelligent and loving way, clearly and unequivocally condemn homosexuality. The response of the Christian on the issue of homosexuality should not be one of emotional trauma toward the repulsion and stigma attached to the movement and its adherents. It should rather be a clear exposition of what the Bible has to say on the subject, with redemptive goals that have clear ramifications for society and the church.

Richard Lovelace, church historian at Gordon-Conwell Theological Seminary in Massachusetts, raises the issue of the church's prophetic responsibility.

> The moral drift argument also misconstrues the role of the church as a prophetic initiator of value-changes within a society. The church has a role to call people to repentance from personal and social sin. The moral drift is probably the result of the church's long silence on personal moral issues and its adjustment to what it has been afraid to change. Some youth workers today elect to hand out contraceptives to high schoolers rather than call them to repentant faith

[14]"Consultation on Homosexuality," unpublished monograph (Cincinnati: College Hill Presbyterian Church, n.d.), p. 7.

> in Christ. A church willing to accept this kind of
> spiritual leadership deserves it.
>
> Another mistake is to think the forces working
> for liberation in our society require and deserve
> the support of the church in the cause of gay
> liberation, just as the parallel instances of the
> civil rights and feminist movements. This ap-
> proach makes the error of lumping together all
> movements of social change in our culture as
> equally representative of God's liberating
> movement in history.[15]

I agree with the biblical model of the preacher as a
prophet proclaiming God's Word in relation to social
issues. The matter of homosexuality in North American society today is not a question of *civil rights*.
Behind civil law is natural law that pre-empts the
laws of men. For example, parental control of children is not a civil right, it is a God-given right brought
about by the natural relationship of parents and children in the God-designed process of procreation. No
civil right or law is "legal" for the Christian if it
contradicts the law of God (Acts 4:18-20).

Furthermore, the matter of "gay liberation" is not
an issue of *human rights*. No one properly functioning as a Christian refuses to recognize God-ordained
human rights, regardless of race, color, or natural
sex. The church has been guilty of violating human
rights in the past, but the homosexuality question is
hardly an example.

Perhaps I take slight exception with the Save Our
Children movement when I suggest that the "gay
rights" drive is not really an issue of *child recruit-*

[15]"How Evangelicals Should Respond to the Homosexual
Issue," *Evangelical Newsletter*, vol. 4, no. 19 (23 September
1977): 4.

ment. This is a horrendous problem and the condemnation is probably supported by the evidence, but child recruitment for homosexual purposes is a symptom, not a cause; it is a side effect, not the real quagmire.

An interesting pamphlet issued by the American Institute of Family Relations asks the question, "Are Homosexuals Necessary?" The Christian is faced with the issue of whether homosexuality is a legitimate life-style, or sickness, or sin. While it is true that the American Psychological Association views homosexuality as a form of mental illness,[16] not all of their members are in agreement with the official line of the organization.

The pamphlet referred to above makes reference to a volume by Dr. Lawrence J. Hatterer of the Payne Whitney Psychiatric Clinic in New York City. Hatterer is also an associate professor at the Cornell University Medical School. In response to the question, "Why change the homosexual," Hatterer replies:

> For the same reason that society tries to change other persons who are sick with a dangerous communicable disease. This, of course, is the point on which violent hostility comes from the professional propagandists who claim that they are just as good as anyone else if not better. But the committee on public health of the New York Academy of Medicine, after a long investigation, declared that homosexuality is "an illness of social proportions, national significance, and serious portent."[17]

[16]Paul Chance and Evelyn Hooker, "Facts That Liberated the Gay Community," *Psychology Today* (December 1975): 12.

[17]Are Homosexuals Necessary?" American Institute of Family Relations, no. 542, p. 1.

Ultimately, the issue is a matter of *sin and righteousness*. The evangelical church has no quarrel with the person who admits homosexual propensity, wants to be relieved of the problem, and is quite willing to repent of the sin of his acts—if any have been committed. However, this action is a defiance of the very definition of "gay." It is the blatant, publicly militant homosexual wishing to force his deviations on society who comes under the condemnation of Scripture and is therefore judged by theological rather than psychological measures. And it is for that strategic reason that the major thrust of this volume is directed toward a treatment of the biblical issues involved.

The forces of truth and the forces of error are lined up on the issue, even though the mix may seem strange with many religionists supporting the gay rights movement. How is that possible? It is really quite simple: One's position on homosexuality is in direct, positive correlation with one's view of Scripture. It is virtually impossible to be committed to a verbally inspired, inerrant, and authoritative Word of God and support the validity of homosexuality as a life-style. It boils down to one simple question: Do you believe the Bible?

Of course some homosexuals who want to find biblical support for their positions will immediately point to the relationship between Jesus and John, or better yet, between David and Jonathan. The so-called "theology of homosexuality" rests upon passages like this as well as a reinterpretation of standard passages that we will look at in later chapters. Gays love to pounce upon a verse like 1 Samuel 20:41 that tells us that David and Jonathan "kissed one another, and wept with one another . . ." (RSV). On another occasion, David tells Jonathan, "very pleasant have you been to me; your love to me was wonderful, passing the love of women" (2 Sam. 1:26, RSV).

However, there is an enormous difference between homosexuality and friendship. There is no indication whatsoever of sexual relationships between either of the two sets of friends mentioned above—or between Ruth and Naomi or Paul and Timothy to add other commonly mentioned Bible characters. The Bible encourages Christians to love each other in a genuine way—men loving men and women loving women—as well as to love in a way that transcends the boundaries of sex.

This is the agape of God, the fruit of the Spirit, the same love that Jesus showed in dying on the cross for a hopeless world. Only a perversion of Scripture can create from this kind of love some implication of physical or sexual relationships. C. S. Lewis dealt with this problem in his famous book *The Four Loves*.

This imposes on me at the outset a very tiresome bit of demolition. It has actually become necessary in our time to rebut the theory that every firm and serious friendship is really homosexual.

The dangerous word *really* is here important. To say that every friendship is consciously and explicitly homosexual would be too obviously false; the wiseacres take refuge in the less palpable charge that it is *really*—unconsciously, cryptically, in some Pickwickian sense— homosexual. And this, though it cannot be proved, can never of course be refuted. The fact that no positive evidence of homosexuality can be discovered in the behavior of two friends does

not disconcert the wiseacres at all: "That," they
say gravely, "is just what we should expect."[18]

The next six chapters will offer a spotlight of
exegesis and interpretation on the major passages in
the Old and New Testaments that deal with the matter of homosexuality. We might as well start right at
the beginning—Sodom.

[18]*The Four Loves* (London: Fontana Books, 1960), pp. 57–58.

CHAPTER 2

THE CRY OF SODOM AND GOMORRAH

Ten books of the Bible (six in the Old Testament and four in the New) offer us clear-cut information on God's view of homosexuality. To be sure, some want to relegate the law of Moses or perhaps even the teaching of the apostle Paul to a cultural application, thereby expressing the view that times have changed and now we really know more about the biological and psychological make-up of human beings.

Such a commitment to a relative point of view is not acceptable to genuine evangelicals. The Christian must recognize that absolute truth as found in God's special revelation, the Bible, invariably leads to absolute values and, therefore, to absolute morality. Time and cultural mores indeed change, but the Bible is transcultural and its truth is as relevant for society today as it was in the past.

> And the Lord said, Because the cry of Sodom and Gomorrah is great, and because their sin is very grievous; I will go down now, and see whether they have done altogether according to the cry of it, which is come unto me; and if not, I will know (Gen. 18:20,21).

> And there came two angels to Sodom at even; and Lot sat in the gate of Sodom: and Lot seeing them rose up to meet them; and he bowed himself with his face toward the ground; And he said, Behold now, my lords, turn in, I pray you, into your servant's house, and tarry all night, and wash your feet, and ye shall rise up early, and go on your ways. And they said, Nay; but we will abide in the street all night. And he pressed upon them greatly; and they turned in unto him, and entered into his house; and he made them a feast, and did bake unleavened bread, and they did eat. But before they lay down, the men of the city, even the men of Sodom, compassed the house round, both old and young, all the people from every quarter: And they called unto Lot, and said unto him, Where are the men which came in to thee this night? bring them out unto us, that we may know them (Gen. 19:1-5).

The story of Sodom and Gomorrah is so linked with homosexuality that "sodomy" has become a synonym for the word in our society. The scriptural passage is actually as clear as it could possibly be Heterosexuality certainly still existed in Sodom, but sexual recreation was rampant in the city to the point that gay crowds roamed the streets demanding sexual relations with every stranger who visited town

Archaeological Evidence

The Genesis account of Sodom and Gomorrah describes the area south of the Dead Sea as a lush valley with rivers and tar pits. Abraham's nephew Lot settled at first outside the city but later moved into the mainstream of Sodomite society. According to the biblical record, God severely judged these two cities and the surrounding area with a rain of fire from heaven.

> Then *Yahweh* made brimstone and fire to rain upon Sodom and Gomorrah, even from *Yahweh*, out of heaven; thus he proceeded to overthrow these cities, and the produce of the ground. Now his wife proceeded to look back; therefore she came to be a pillar of salt. When Abraham rose up early in the morning to the place where he had stood before *Yahweh*, he proceeded to look down upon Sodom and Gomorrah and upon all the land of the valley and to observe, and behold the smoke of the land went up like the smoke of a furnace (Gen. 19:24-28).[1]

Did such a judgmental catastrophe ever happen? The present geography of the area seems to support the record of cataclysmic destruction. At the southern end of the Dead Sea variable heights of the same rock strata on the west, east, and south ends seem to confirm the account. These are made up of lower Cretaceous or Nubian sandstone built upon a layer of Cambrian. The fault at either side of the Dead Sea indicates an earthquake. Sulphur-marl nodules found in the faults could very well be related to what the Bible calls "brimstone," which is also referred to as 'the rock that burns—sulphur." The mound of salt, which is 150 feet thick at places, is called "Mount Sodom" by present-day Israelis.

The area surrounding this portion of the Dead Sea is useless because of salt on its surface. Israel annually reclaims 250 thousand tons of potash from the southern part of the Dead Sea, which is only fifteen

[1]J.W. Watts, *A Distinctive Translation of Genesis* (Grand Rapids: Eerdmans, 1963), p. 54.

feet deep south of the Lisan jutting into the Dead Sea's eastern shore.

Archaeologist Nelson Glueck has identified over four hundred village sites in Northern Negev, most of them last inhabited about 2000 to 1800 b.c. Today archaeologists are uncovering ruins of a vast civilization in the ancient Sodom-Gomorrah valley. Under water archaeologists claim they have identified forms similar to foundations of ancient cities in the southern end of the Dead Sea.[2]

One of these underwater archaeologists is Ralph E. Baney whose work has been documented by K. O Emery of the University of Southern California in a monograph entitled "A Reconnaissance Study of the Floor of the Dead Sea." Though not even listed in J. A. Thompson's famous *Archaeology*, Sodom has become the subject of significant recent research in archaeology, and Baney is quite convinced that his expeditions using caisson construction equipment will "reveal something of the culture and mores of those Biblical days and thus humbly verify the Scrip tural account of God's destruction by fire and brimstone of the wicked cities of Sodom and Gomor rah.[3]

Whether or not the actual ruins of Sodom and Gomorrah will ever be found and clearly identified is not the point. It is quite obvious that professional archaeologists have confirmed the cataclysmic experiences of the area. As early as 1924, Melvin G. Kyle, then president of Xenia Theological Seminary, attempted to unearth the sites of the two cities. As a

[2]Ibid.
[3]Adapted from an unpublished outline on the Archaeology of Sodom and Gomorrah developed by Dr. Mary Stanton and based upon Baly's *Geography of the Bible* and the *Encyclopedia of Geomorphology* by Fairbridge.

result of that expedition, Kyle was able to state that 'there is now scientific evidence that the civilization which the Bible represents to have been on this plain in the days of Abraham and Lot, and of Sodom and Gomorrah, was actually here.''[4]

Later the Standard Oil Company discovered oil in the region, and geologists state that with oil and asphalt there will also be highly flammable gases. The Book of Genesis does speak of slime pits (*bitumen,* Gen. 14:10) and some have speculated that lightning or some other God-initiated agent ignited a large pocket of gas that literally blew up the valley, and the very large quantities of sulphur and salt found in the area were carried red hot into the heavens so that it literally rained fire and brimstone! This is not to suggest that the destruction of Sodom and Gomorrah was not miraculous, for without question it was. But who is to say what precise means God used to accomplish His judgment of the area?[5]

Degradation of Canaanite Religions

It is impossible to separate our study of homosexuality and the sin of Sodom from the status of Canaanite religions in the days of Abraham and Lot. Merrill F. Unger has written precisely what it was like:

In their religion the Canaanites were enslaved by one of the most terrible and degrading forms of idolatry, which abetted rather than restrained their immorality. That Canaan's curse was basi-

[4]Arthur C. Custance, "Some Remarkable Biblical Confirmations from Archaeology with Special Emphasis on the Book of Genesis," *Dorway Paper,* no. 39 (Ottawa, Canada, 1963), p. 20.
[5]Ibid.

cally religious has been amply demonstrated by archaeology, particularly by the discovery of the Canaanite religious texts from the ancient Ugarit in North Syria, 1929-1937. These texts fully corroborate the estimate of such older scholars as Lenormant, who said of Canaanite religion, "No other people ever rivaled them in the mixture of bloodshed and debauchery with which they thought to honor the Diety."[6]

More particularly on the subject of Sodom, Unger noted:

The goddess was called *Qudshu*, "The Holiness," that is, "The Holy One," in the perverted moral sense, and representations of her as a nude woman bestride a lion with a lily in one hand and a serpent in the other, point her out as a divine courtesan. In the same sense, the male prostitutes consecrated to the cult of *Qudshu* and prostituting themselves to her honor, were called *Qadesh*, usually translated "Sodomites" (Deuteronomy 23:18; 1 Kings 14:24; 15:12; 22:46). The feminine *Qedeshah* is also found (Deuteronomy 23:18; Hosea 4:14).[7]

It is important to grasp the general paganism of the surrounding area in order to better understand how theologically significant the sin of Sodom was. The desecration to the unnatural vice was hardly restricted to Sodom and Gomorrah, though these may have been its center of activity. It was spread in various forms over Phoenicia, Syria, Phrygia, Assyria, and Babylonia throughout the following years.

[6]*Archaeology and the Old Testament* (Grand Rapids: Zondervan, 1954), p. 75.
[7]Ibid., pp. 173–74.

Later Ashtoreth (the Greek Astarte) became its chief object and the worship centered in a group of emasculated priests of Cybele called Galli who all apparently took their cue from early Canaanite paganism in Sodom.

What Was the Sin of Sodom?

Weak protests have been raised against the historic understanding of the Sodom account on the basis that the Hebrew verb *yoda* ("to know") does not necessarily mean sexual knowledge. Exegetes sympathizing with the gay position have suggested that perhaps the Sodomites really only wanted to get acquainted with Lot's guests. The position is so futile it is hardly worth answering since the word "know" is a common Bible euphemism for sexual relations, and anything short of the use of *yoda* in this particular passage leaves completely unexplained why the men were willing to break down the door and injure Lot in order to be hospitable and shake hands with his guests.

In addition, such an interpretation offers no reasons why Lot felt compelled to offer his daughters to the ravenous crowd outside the door. J. H. Hertz, the late chief rabbi of the British Empire, could hardly have been accused of being a fundamentalist Christian, but in his commentary on the Sodom and Gomorrah account, he articulated lucidly the basic Judeo-Christian interpretation of the passage by saying that emphasis is here laid on the fact that the inhabitants were all addicted to unnatural depravity.

To be sure, there were other sins in Sodom as there have been in every city of every nation throughout all the times of man. But we know of only one episode in history where God singled out a particular sin and destroyed two entire cities because of it—the sin was homosexuality and the cities were Sodom and Gomorrah.

But, of course, "gay theologians" do not agree. The classic work offering a gay exegesis of Genesis 19 was written in 1955 by Anglican scholar Derrick Bailey (see critical review in Appendix 1). Entitled *Homosexuality in the Western Christian Tradition* (Longman's, 1955; reprint by Archon Books, 1975), Bailey's book argues that a great deal of Christian prejudice against homosexuality is a result of a misunderstanding of the Sodom account, which he sees as one dealing not with sexual immorality, but with social customs of the city. It appears that Lot had angered the residents of Sodom by receiving foreigners whose credentials had not been examined. Terribly upset by this social injustice, the men were pounding at Lot's door demanding to see those credentials. The "sin of Sodom" therefore was inhospitality. Bailey's position has been expounded by Ralph Blair.

> In this story Lot provides food and shelter for two strangers—actually angels. During the evening, all the men of the city surround Lot's house and demand that the two men be given over to them. Lot bargains with the mob and agrees to release to them his two virgin daughters since the two strangers had come "under the shelter of my roof." The angry mob starts to attack Lot and he escapes back into his house. The two guests then strike the mob blind. In none of the early rabbinical commentaries is there the slightest hint of a "homosexual" interpretation to the story of the sin of Sodom. The "homosexual" rendering derives from later Greek influences, particularly the writings of Philo and Josephus (c.f. e.g.,

Bailey, p. 10ff). The Biblical story demonstrates the seriousness with which these early Eastern people took the important customs of Oriental hospitality. It appears that, if necessary, they would even allow their own daughters to undergo abuse in order to protect guests. The sexual aspect of the story is simply the vehicle in which the subject of demanded hospitality is conveyed. As it is clearly interpreted in Ezekiel 16:49: "Behold, this was the guilt of your sister Sodom: she and her daughters had pride, surfeit of food, and prosperous ease, but did not aid the poor and needy." Evangelical references to the sin of Sodom in their concentration on the scene at Lot's door and the "homosexual" explanation completely overlook Ezekiel and the Biblical fact that God had already declared Sodom to be grievously sinful before the incident at Lot's house (Genesis 18:20).[8]

We'll examine the Ezekiel account later, but let us not be so naive as to suggest that any evangelical scholar thinks homosexuality all of a sudden exploded in Sodom at Lot's door. Of course God had already declared Sodom to be grievously sinful—its homosexuality had sent up a stench for years. Abraham had been told that the destruction would take place before the angels even entered the city.

The real argument centers on the word *yoda*. Bailey argued that he could find only fifteen examples of the word used in a sexual sense in the Old Testament and more than nine hundred examples

[8]"An Evangelical Look at Homosexuality" (Originally published as "The Gay Evangelical"), *Homosexuality and Religion*, no. 13. (n.p.: 1972): 4. Published as part of the monograph series of the National Task Force on Student Personnel Service and Homosexuality.

where it was used in the primary sense of having a *mental understanding*. But an exegete is not impressed by such statistics since interpretation based on the contextual argument is always stronger. Even if there were just one or two other uses of *yoda* used in the Scripture in a clearly sexual sense, we would certainly be led to a conclusion of its sexual emphasis in this passage. Derek Kidner has rebutted Bailey's argument quite adequately.

> To this we may reply: (a) statistics are no substitute for contextual evidence (otherwise the rarer sense of the word would never seem probable), and in both these passages the demand to "know" is used in its sexual sense (Genesis 19:8; Judges 19:25). Even apart from this verbal conjunction it would be grotesquely inconsequent that Lot should reply to a demand for credentials by an offer of daughters; (b) Psychology can suggest how "to know" acquired its secondary sense; but in fact, the use of the word is completely flexible. No one suggests that in Judges 19:25 the men of Gibeah were gaining "knowledge" of their victim in the sense of personal relationship, yet "know" is the word used of them; (c) Conjecture here has the marks of special pleading, for it substitutes a trivial reason ("commotion . . . inhospitality") for a serious one, for it is silenced by Jude 7, a pronouncement which Dr. Bailey has to discount as belonging to a late stage of interpretation.[9]

Whatever the record of the rabbinical commentaries, the history of evangelical scholarship has

[9]*Genesis* (Downers Grove, Ill.: InterVarsity Press, 1967), p. 49.

hardly wavered on the sin of Sodom. The great Lutheran scholar H. C. Leupold said it this way:

> *There is hardly a more horrible account anywhere in the pages of Holy Writ. Both the degeneracy here described as well as the catastrophic overthrow of the cities involved are calculated to startle by their lewd and gruesome details. Luther confessed that he could not read the chapter without a feeling of deep revulsion ....
> ....
> The enormity of the prevalent vice was indicated by the fact that the sacred duty of hospitality was so completely replaced by the eagerness to practice vile lust that even strangers would be sacrificed to wholesale abuse—a treatment most likely to terminate in death. The events of this evening display a shocking depravity. The facts of the case are now apparent to all the world whether these people "have done altogether according to the cry" which had come unto the Lord. The euphemism, "that we may know them" (nedhe'ah), is not born out of delicacy, for they shout forth their libidinous desires aloud in the streets of the city (c.f., Isaiah 3:9; Judges 19:22).[10]

Lot's Role in the City

The significance of Lot "sitting in the gate of Sodom" is not just a casual reference to the place he spent his leisure time. It is rather a specific description of the official meeting place of the elders where legal matters were dealt with and political affairs discussed. It is quite possible that Lot took advan-

[10]*Exposition of Genesis*, reprint ed. (Grand Rapids: Baker Book House, 1956), pp. 554, 558.

tage of his role in order to be of use to good men who entered this wicked city. Let us give him the benefit of the doubt. That would account for his immediate response to the angels in the early verses of Genesis 19.

And we should note that Lot's hospitality in insisting they spend the night in his house rather than out in the open was no mere Oriental gesture—regardless of how seriously these ancients took their customs of kindness to strangers. He knew full well the danger awaiting them in his own city.

One wonders, of course, how "just Lot" (2 Pet. 2:7), a man declared by Scripture to be righteous in his heart, could stand the rottenness of the cesspool in which he lived. Donald Barnhouse raised essentially the same question.

> How could Lot have any affection for a place where the inhabitants were so filthily depraved as to come to his door at night seeking to vent their depravity upon his guests? How could a just man linger in a city where he had almost been forced to sacrifice the honor of his daughters? It is an amazing picture of the lust of the flesh against a drawing of the Spirit. Any man who thinks that his fleshly appetites will be stilled while he is on earth has not comprehended the baseness of Lot's desires, nor, indeed, his own.[11]

Contemporary friends of the homosexual move ment would do well to note the *depths of backsliding* to which Lot had fallen. Apparently he could comfortably overlook the sin of the city until it affected his own house and the guests for whom he was directly responsible.

[11]*Genesis, A Devotional Commentary* (Grand Rapids: Zon dervan, 1970), p. 163.

The Importance of Ezekiel 16:48,49

As I live, saith the Lord God, Sodom thy sister hath not done, she nor her daughters, as thou hast done, thou and thy daughters. Behold, this was the iniquity of thy sister Sodom, pride, fulness of bread, and abundance of idleness was in her and in her daughters, neither did she strengthen the hand of the poor and needy (Ezek. 16:48,49).

Why didn't the prophet deal with the notorious atrocities that have made Sodom a symbol of degradation for centuries? Partly because his purpose here was to compare Jerusalem with Samaria and Sodom. He therefore selected those elements of evil common to all three, and the former two were not to be compared to Sodom in sexual perversion. Selfishness and pride *were* sins of Sodom, but the verse hardly claims they were her *only* sins. *The Pulpit Commentary* suggests that "the prophet fixes on the point which made Sodom a luxurious and sensual city, the graver evil being just hinted at in the word abominations, and as the outcome of the evil tendencies."[12]

Furthermore, a focus only on verse 49 fails again to take into consideration the total contextual argument. The proverb begins at verse 44 and continues through 59. Sodom is mentioned not once, but five times in the passage. In addition to pride, fulness of bread, abundance of idleness, and a failure to strengthen the hand of the poor and needy, also mentioned are such terms as "abomination," "shame," "wickedness," and "lewdness." Matthew Henry wrote that Sodom's most flagrant wickedness (i.e. going after strange flesh) "is not mentioned, because

[12]*The Pulpit Commentary,* Ezekiel, vol. 1, H.D.M. Spence and J.S. Excell, eds. (London: Funk and Wagnalls, n.d.), p. 300.

notoriously known; but those sins which did not look so black, but opened the door and led the way to these more enormous crimes, and began to fill that measure of her sins, which was filled up at length by their unnatural filthiness." [13]

Two Helpful New Testament Passages

Second Peter 2 and Jude 7 cannot be dismissed in our attempt to better understand the Sodom account in the Book of Genesis.

> if he condemned the cities of Sodom and Gomorrah by burning them to ashes, and made them an example of what is going to happen to the ungodly; . . . then the Lord knows how to rescue godly men from trials and to hold the unrighteous for the day of judgment, while continuing their punishment (2 Pet. 2:6,9; NIV).

> In a similar way, Sodom and Gomorrah and the surrounding towns gave themselves up to sexual immorality and perversion. They serve as an example of those who suffer the punishment of eternal fire (Jude 7, NIV).

The region of the southern part of the Dead Sea stands forever as a warning of God's judgment against the iniquity of Sodom and Gomorrah. The destruction of the two cities was a catastrophic demonstration that God cannot tolerate such behavior indefinitely. The Jude passage is even stronger than 2 Peter, stating the sin of Sodom as involving "sexual immorality" *(ekporneuo)* and "perversion" *(sarkos*

---

[13]*An Exposition of the Old and New Testament,* vol. 3 (Old Tappan, N.J.: Fleming H. Revell, n.d.), p. 556.

heteras). It is simply sophomoric exegesis to apply this kind of language description of Sodom's sin to anything other than rampant homosexuality. The emphasis is on extravagant and unbridled lust—Lot knew it, Abraham knew it, God knew it, and we had better understand it in our day.

So the rampant wickedness of men with respect to sexual deviation had to be dealt with in the Law. God could not form an organized nation on the shoulders of relativistic thinkers like Lot. In view of the Book of Genesis, it is not surprising that we find frequent references to sexual deviation in the Mosaic Law

CHAPTER 3

HOMOSEXUALITY AND THE MOSAIC LAW

Sinai—from 1450 B.C. to the present—this stretch of seemingly endless desert continues to be an unlikely focal point for the world's attention. In general, the term applies to a dusty peninsula that lies south of the wilderness of Paran between the Gulf of Aqabah and Suez. It is roughly triangular in shape and about 150 miles wide at the north end. The distance north and south is about 250 miles punctuated about two-thirds of the way down and midway between Aqabah and Suez by *Jebel Mūsa,* the mountain of Moses where tradition tells us the Law was given.

Though the Scriptures state that the Law was given on Mount Sinai, there is a great deal of debate among archaeologists over the exact location of the mountain. One cartographer says of the traditional area

> that the more southerly, greater height of the range, the *Jebel Mūsa,* was identified with Sinai suggests that it had already enjoyed special sanctity in pre-Christian times. The mere fact that its view lies open to the distant *et Tīh,* could well suggest to those who saw it from some northerly

vantage point, or knew of its existence in that mysterious pocket, that it was, indeed, the Holy mount. Robinson's characterization of *Rās Safsafeh* applies even better to *Jebel Mūsa:* "This adytum in the midst of the great circular granite region, with only a single feasible entrance; a secret holy place shut out from the world amid lone and desolate mountains."[1]

But the location of the mountain is not our primary concern. What does concern us is a series of laws given there in approximately 1450 B.C. These were not laws derived by the ancients from some council meeting over which Moses presided, but the very Word of God given directly to His servant at Sinai.

Thou shalt not lie with mankind, as with womankind: it is abomination. Neither shalt thou lie with any beast to defile thyself therewith: neither shall any woman stand before a beast to lie down thereto: it is confusion. Defile not ye yourselves in any of these things: for in all these the nations are defiled which I cast out before you (Lev. 18:22-24).

If a man also lie with mankind, as he lieth with a woman, both of them have committed an abomination: they shall surely be put to death; their blood shall be upon them (Lev. 20:13).

There shall be no whore of the daughters of Israel, nor a sodomite of the sons of Israel. Thou shalt not bring the hire of a whore, or the price of a dog, into the house of the Lord thy God for any vow: for even both these are abomination unto the Lord thy God (Deut. 23:17,18).

[1]Emil G. Kraeling, *Bible Atlas* (Chicago: Rand McNally, 1956), p. 113.

Why the specificity of these injunctions against homosexuality? Again the answer cannot be understood apart from an understanding of the land to which the Israelites were headed at that time. The entire Mosaic Law was geared to helping God's people live pure lives, both in an individual and national sense, when surrounded by the corruption of the Canaanites.

Corruption in Canaan

No doubt the Israelites who were being instructed in the Law at Sinai knew well the historic record of Lot and his family at Sodom and Gomorrah. We can be sure that Israeli parents drilled their children through the years in Egypt in all the detailed history of the patriarchs and how God had dealt with them—both in blessing and punishment. There is no way they could have known, however, what lay ahead in the vile cesspool called Canaan. Sodom and Gomorrah had been destroyed, but their influence lived on and would soon be thrust before God's people at every turn. James Kelso has reminded us:

> The immorality displayed in the Sodom and Gomorrah episode is typical of Canaanite religion. Since the highest gods of the Canaanites went in for immorality, their worshippers naturally did so also. Sex orgies were common and the temples had their male and female prostitutes. And along with these were self-made eunuch priests and a guild of homosexuals.[2]

The wretched worship of idols was bad enough, but these particular idols in Canaan were representa-

[2]*Archaeology and the Ancient Testament* (Grand Rapids: Zondervan, 1968), pp. 55–56.

tive of a new low in Jewish experience. Baal, who haunted the Israelites right up to the time of their captivity, was worshipped as the storm god, and as the giver of rain, functioned as a fertility deity. Three major godesses—Astarte, Anath, and Asherah—were really "sex goddesses" functioning both as mother goddesses and sacred prostitutes with an emphasis on the latter role. Sexual defilement has always posed a common and ready sin trap for the people of God from the Book of Genesis to the present. What the Canaanites had done was to fashion gods after their own lustful, human image, a striking contrast to Yahweh who was neither god nor goddess, infinitely beyond gender, and never to be associated with anything human except in His own divinely designed theophanies and finally in the incarnate Son.

It could well be that the homosexual practices rampant in Canaan were a part of the worship of Astarte or Ashtoreth. This would fit in well with the idea of both male and female temple prostitution. Those who argue that homosexual practices can be traced to religious worship down through the years are entirely right. But that religious worship is clearly a deliberate and complete defilement of what the God of heaven intended.

Homosexuality and Capital Punishment

Gay religionists attack these Scripture passages by reminding us that few evangelical leaders opposing the homosexual advance would recommend the death penalty for practicing homosexuals and, therefore, conclude that none of the passage is really relevant to the contemporary scene. To be sure, there are other prohibitions in the Levitical code no one would think of requiring today because they have been superseded or abolished under the new covenant. But Harold Lindsell succinctly explains why that argument does not apply to the Leviticus passage.

> The answer is plain. The New Testament (and thus the new covenant, which speaks to the people of God in this age of the Church, and of the Holy Spirit) also condemns homosexuality while it does not repeat nor advocate some of the other prohibitions of the old covenant. Paul declares that homosexuals shall not inherit the Kingdom of God (1 Corinthians 6:9,10).[3]

It is precisely this matter of the death penalty that causes some well-meaning theologians great difficulty with the passages banning homosexuality. This is particularly true of liberals, however, who are quite willing to take a less-than-authoritative view of Scripture. Helmut Thielicke saws an old board when he raises again the questions with which I dealt in the last chapter regarding the essence of sodomy as it was practiced in the ancient cities.

> As far as the *Old Testament* is concerned, it is uncertain whether the passages concerning "sodomy," which have been traditionally authoritative, actually refer to homosexual acts at all. In any case, Isaiah 1:10,23, Ezekiel 16:49, and Jeremiah 23:14 characterize the sins that were responsible for the downfall of Sodom quite differently. Apart from this there can be no doubt that the Old Testament regarded homosexuality and pederasty as crimes punishable by death (Leviticus 18:22, 20:13). Whether direct injunc-

[3]"Homosexuals and the Church," *Christianity Today* (28 September 1973): 10.

tions are to be derived from this for Christians
must remain a matter of discussion, at least in-
sofar as behind this prohibition there lies the
concept of cultic defilement and thus the question is raised whether and to what extent the Old
Testament cultic law can be binding upon those
who are under the Gospel and to what extent it
places them on a wholly new level and frees them
from the Law.[4]

Advocates and opponents of homosexual practice
are agreed on one thing—the Old Testament Law
does require the death penalty for the practice of
homosexuality. To us in our "enlightened" society,
capital punishment prescribed for the breaking of
sexual laws is unthinkable. And to be sure, there was
a cultural application in the days of the Old Testament. One writer suggests that the penalty was an
attempt to preserve the monotheistic ideal and was
therefore far more related to religious practice than
to the associated sexual behaviors.[5]

Others think that God was concerned about the
protection of the ongoing separated community and
that the death penalty was justified because of the
fact that incest, adultery, and homosexuality are tan-
tamount to the murder of family life.

But Thielicke's question has not been answered
with respect to the new covenant. Even if the death
penalty was justified to maintain the purity of the
nation of Israel in the Canaanite context, wouldn't
that be completely set aside by the gospel of grace?
This is precisely the point Clinton Jones throws at us,

[4]*The Ethics of Sex* (New York: Harper & Row, 1964), pp.
277–78.
[5]E. Neufeld, *Ancient Hebrew Marriage Laws* (London: Green
& Co., 1944), p. 11.

using as his New Testament illustration the dialog between Jesus and the woman taken in adultery.

> With regard to homosexuality and the Bible, many people are aware of the law in Leviticus: "You shall not lie with a male as with a woman; it is an abomination" and "whoever shall do any of these abominations . . . shall be cut off from among their people" (Leviticus 18:22,29). But the Old Testament penalty for homosexuality is no more severe than that for a long list of other offenses. Churchgoers must be familiar with what Jesus said about the woman taken in adultery: "Let him who is without sin among you be the first to throw a stone at her" and ". . . go, and do not sin again." (John 8:7,11). Thus the adulterer is punished by death in the Old Testament but receives forgiveness from Jesus. Is there any reason to believe that homosexual behavior would not have received mercy and forgiveness in the same way?[6]

Here Jones has unwittingly tipped his hand. To be sure, the thinking Christian would not argue for an application of the Levitical law of stoning for either adultery or homosexuality. But the parallel that Jones himself draws is precisely the point evangelicals are attempting to make regarding homosexuality. Jesus referred to the woman's adultery as *sin* and admonished her to *cease from sinning.*
It is not a question of punishment, but rather a question of confession, i.e., the admission of homosexuality as sin, that is at the crux of the whole problem. Of course the answer to Jones's last question is a strong affirmative. Certainly, the committed

[6]*Homosexuality and Counseling* (Philadelphia: Fortress Press, 1974), p. 11.

Christian believes that homosexual behavior can receive "mercy and forgiveness," but first there must be a recognition of that behavior as sin and a willingness to receive the mercy and forgiveness—as well as a willingness to apply the admonition to "go and sin no more."

So Jones is no help at all to Bailey and Blair who argue that ritual purity and moral preaching are assumed to be always distinct. Another exegete uses the same reasoning in attributing the passages in the Book of Leviticus to a "priestly compiler."

> The epilogue (18:22-30) highlights the ritual disqualification effected not only by the five acts so condemned, but by all 17 listed. The notion of becoming ceremonially unclean (T.M.'N) is used once in the (second) list of seven prohibited acts (18:17-23) but no fewer than six times in the epilogue (cf. 18:20 with 18:24,25,27,28,30); a notion of abomination (to'egah), which is used once in the list 18:17-23 for male homosexual acts occurs four times in the epilogue (cf. 18:22 with 18:26,27,29,30). This shows that the priestly compiler wished to bring these matters up-to-date by augmenting the inherited list (18:7-16) with the various prohibitions of 18:17-23. He also qualified all prohibitions similarly as "abominations" which make one "ceremonially unclean." For him the amended list in 18:6-23 now both summarizes and exemplifies what denies or destroys Israel's identity as a religious group.[7]

But to view the prohibitions against homosexuality strictly as a concern for involvement in alien religions is to suggest that Leviticus 18 teaches only ritual

[7]Wolfgang Roth, "What of Sodom and Gomorrah?" *Explor 1* (Fall 1975): 10.

purity and not ethical or moral purity as well. Blair emphasizes the priest's concern for the former and the prophet's concern for the latter.

No doubt cultic and moral purity do often coincide, but to apply such a principle throughout Scripture would lead to very difficult conclusions. Is adultery merely a ritual wrong without concern for moral implications? Is child sacrifice only a matter of cultic concern? Is there nothing inherently evil with bestiality?

But the major problem with the way gay exegetes treat the Mosaic Law is their lack of concern for absolute divine revelation. Here again is Blair:

> From the priestly point of view, it is clear that above all else Israel was to be uncontaminated by her pagan neighbors. In all things, she was to remain a separate, "pure vessel unto the Lord." At this time, male prostitutes in the temples of the Canaanites, Babylonians, and other neighboring peoples were common features of the pagan rites. Therefore, it is understandable that this "homosexuality" connected with the worship of false gods would certainly color Israel's perspective on any and all homosexual activity.[8]

The implication is clear—Israel was against homosexuality only because the Canaanites and Babylonians were doing it. The commanded separation was not primarily a separation from sin and evil, but more an ethnic and religious separation from the practices of the pagan Canaanites.

But our texts in Leviticus are a classic example that Israel's history represents a zealous ethnic purity based on moral imperatives of divine will revealed

---

[8]Blair, "Evangelical Look at Homosexuality": 3.

through the righteousness of the Law. In Leviticus 18:4,5 we hear God say "my judgments" and "my statutes." God judged Israel as He judges us on the basis of moral right and wrong based upon absolute standards of righteousness revealed through the Law, the prophets, and all other Bible writers.

The *coup de grace* to the arguments of Blair and Bailey is the fact that condemnations against homosexual behavior are repeated in the New Testament (as we shall see in later chapters). Burl De-Long states it well:

> So the proscriptions of Leviticus 18:23 and 20:13 are still highly relevant, not because they are in the law of Moses, but because they have been reincorporated into the New Testament ethic. Therefore, while Christians need not look to the Old Testament as the basis of their authority today, evangelicals still have the right to point to it as an authority in the present discussion. It is unfair and illogical to chide or accuse evangelicals of using Leviticus in a selective manner, simply to "reinforce their prejudice." Such an argument is based on emotional appeal and reveals an inability to recognize and understand the progress of revelation and the moral unity between the Old and New Testaments.[9]

What is quite obvious in all of the writings of those who attempt to defend homosexuality from the theological point of view is their complete commitment to relativism. It is impossible to acknowledge the absolutism of biblical norms and also affirm a

[9]"A Critique of Current Evangelical Interpretation Regarding the Biblical Understanding of Homosexuality" (Master's Degree thesis, Dallas Theological Seminary, 1977), pp. 23–24.

validity for homosexual behavior. Blatant relativism is obvious in the writings of Rod Benson.

> Factually, what man does is choose which laws of nature, biological and non-biological, he wishes to operate within at a particular time and place. The more knowledge he accumulates, the more he is able to change the "is" into whatever he desires. So the argument that homosexuality is against the law of nature, that it is perverse, has as much or as little logical and factual substantiation as the assertion that circumcision, bottle feeding, contraception, eating of cooked foods, or mouth genital contact are perverse. Perversity is a term used by those who do not approve of your way of changing or modifying a law of nature. All a person is entitled to say so far in our discussion is: I do not like homosexuality because . . . and here he can supply a reason. However, he cannot say the reason is that it is against the laws of nature (because this is a personal choice of which of nature's laws he would like to be dominant).[10]

Obviously, Benson is not really treating the subject with any theological sensitivity. He is simply saying that what we call "laws of nature" are not really laws, but merely our understanding of the way nature operates in a given place and time. Once again, this is a typical secular commitment to relativism in which religious (and even self-styled evangelical) writers get trapped. "Right" is what people feel is socially acceptable at a given time and "wrong" is what society disapproves at a given time.

The argument is really quite clear: No one can take

[10] *In Defense of Homosexuality* (New York: Julian Press, 1965), p. 21.

a serious view of the authority and inerrancy of Scripture and deny its abhorrence of homosexual behavior. The very term "evangelical acceptance of homosexuality" is a contradiction because the term "evangelical" connotes a serious view of the authority of Scripture, including the Old Testament, which precludes a willingness to accept homosexuality as normal or in any way God-approved.

Hire of a Whore/Price of a Dog

In the Deuteronomic recitation of the Law (Deut. 23:18) we do not see a repetition of the death penalty as it appeared in Leviticus, though without question it still stands. Here Moses gives a new twist from Jehovah that says no son of Israel shall be a "sodomite" and that bringing money gained from "the hire of a whore, or the price of a dog" to the Lord in payment of a vow is completely forbidden because both of these things are an abomination.

Surely we can understand the "hire of a whore" as the practice of prostitution, probably heterosexual. But what does the text mean by "the price of a dog"? Unger has given an idea.

> In Deuteronomy 23:17, the toleration of a sodomite was expressly forbidden, and the pay received by a sodomite was not to be put into the temple treasury (vs. 18). "The price of a dog" is a figurative expression used to denote the gains of a *qadesh* (sodomite), who was called *kinaidos,* by the Greeks, from the doglike manner in which he debased himself (see Revelation 22:15, where the unclean are called "dogs").[11]

[11]*Unger's Bible Dictionary* (Chicago: Moody Press, 1957), p. 35.

The image is an unpleasant one, but we cannot shy away from what Scripture plainly says. An ass could be redeemed by a lamb and the lamb could be sacrificed, but a dog was completely unacceptable. The New Testament speaks of the "dog that turns to his own vomit again" and of such a person the apostle John wrote, "without are dogs, and sorcerers, and whoremongers, and murderers, and idolaters, and whosoever loveth and maketh a lie" (Rev. 22:15).

Such a scriptural designation hardly gives the contemporary Christian a basis for calling homosexuals "dogs" or treating them as such. This kind of attitude on the part of the church is what results in anti-gay crimes like those perpetrated by a new version of the Ku Klux Klan, which reportedly was organized at an Oklahoma City high school in January, 1978. Over one hundred students, mostly ages fifteen and sixteen and from the southwestern part of the city and surrounding suburbs, allegedly used baseball bats to attack patrons at a club that reportedly caters to homosexuals. People have been injured, tires slashed, and cars vandalized by the mobs in recent months.[12]

Is the Mosaic Law important in regard to the question of homosexuality? The apostle Paul thought so when he reminded the Roman Christians that "sin is not taken into account when there is no law" (Rom. 5:13, NIV). But the result of law is grace and the effect of grace is redemption.

> The law was added so that the trespass might increase. But where sin increased, grace increased all the more, so that, just as sin reigned in death, so also grace might reign through righ-

[12]*The Miami Herald,* 27 January 1978, p. 12-A.

teousness to bring eternal life through Jesus Christ our Lord (Rom. 5:20,21; NIV).

And God's grace still abounds toward people in our day, and on precisely the same terms as the Book of Romans identifies. It is this kind of grace that brought a woman named Pam Reston out of a life of lesbianism to membership in the family of God.

Pam came from a very religious background and a church setting that emphasized emotion and experientialism. Out of that context, and indeed while still within it, she gave in to homosexual tendencies and became a practicing lesbian. But Pam is *cured*. By the power of Jesus Christ her life has been transformed and both the practice and propensity of homosexuality have been removed. She is now engaged to be married to a Christian man and is a faithful, active member of an evangelical congregation. Her pastor affirmed this information to me in person.

I include this brief vignette to remind the reader again that the transforming power of Christ extends to the homosexual. Of course there have been those professing conversion and cure but falling back again into old behavioral patterns. That is true of "converted" drunks, thieves, junkies, and liars. But the failure of few or many cannot negate the redemptive potential of the gospel.

CHAPTER 4

TALE OF TWO CITIES

The Book of Judges contains the history of the Israeli theocracy for a period of about three hundred and fifty years from the death of Joshua to the death of Samson, or more properly, to the rise of the prophet Samuel. It was a period of great oppression, alienation from God, and humiliation in the face of enemies. The era was broken by occasional periods of repentance and subsequent righteousness under the leadership of judges God raised up to lead His people.

The particular narrative that concerns us appears in Judges 19. Scholars place this chapter in the early historical period of the judges, immediately following the death of Joshua—a fact that is ascertained by the information that Phinehas (the son of Eleazar who was a contemporary of Joshua) was high priest at the time (20:28). Civil government was in a state of decline and moral leadership was virtually absent.

The plot of the story runs rather like an X-rated movie of the late twentieth century. A Levite, who lived outside of the appointed Levitical towns (most likely in the mountains of Ephraim near Shiloh), took a concubine out of Bethlehem who later proved unfaithful and returned home to her parents. He went after her, reconciled their differences, and after a delay due to a misunderstanding with her parents, he headed north again.

Though it would have been logical in terms of time to stop at Jerusalem, we must remember that the city was still in the hands of the Canaanites and a Levite had no interest in stopping there. So he went on north about twenty furlongs to Gibeah, the city of the tribe of Benjamin, where he entered just as darkness fell and found no one who would offer any hospitality for lodging.

Finally, an old man came in from the fields. He was not really a resident of Gibeah but just living there temporarily. The farmer invited the Levite and his concubine home with him, took care of their animals, and allowed them to rest awhile before they had dinner together.

What happened next is so black in the annals of Jewish history that Josephus could not bring himself to tell the truth about the passage. Here is his revised ersion:

> Now certain young men of the inhabitants of Gibeah, having seen the woman in the marketplace, and admiring her beauty, when they understood that she lodged with the old man, came to the doors, as condemning the weakness and fewness of the old man's family; and when the old man desired them to go away, and not to offer any violence or abuse there, they desired him to yield up the strange woman, and then he should have no harm done to him: and when the old man alleged that the Levite was of his kindred, and that they would be guilty of hard wickedness if they suffered themselves to be overcome by their pleasures and so offend

against their laws, they despised his righteous admonition, and laughed him to scorn.[1]

So much for the protection of the reputation of one's nation at the expense of accurate history. Here is the biblical account taken from the narrative of *The Living Bible:*

> Just as they were beginning to warm to the occasion, a gang of sex perverts gathered around the house and began beating at the door and yelling at the old man to bring out the man who was staying with him, so they could rape him. The old man stepped outside to talk to them. "No, my brothers, don't do such a dastardly act," he begged, "for he is my guest. Here, take my virgin daughter and this man's wife. I'll bring them out and you can do whatever you like to them—but don't do such a thing to this man." But they wouldn't listen to him. Then the girl's husband pushed her out to them, and they abused her all night, taking turns raping her until morning. Finally, just at dawn, they let her go. She fell down at the door of the house and lay there until it was light. When her husband opened the door to be on his way, he found her there, fallen down in front of the door with her hands digging into the threshold (Judg. 19:22-27).

Geographical and Cultural Setting

Gibeah—city of fame and infamy; known most prominently in Scripture as the strong fortress from which the first king ruled Israel; located on the site of modern Tell el-Ful. Saul was born here in this one of fourteen cities of Benjamin located just four miles

[1]*Antiquities of the Jews,* book 5, chapter 2.

north of Jerusalem and two miles south of Ramah, the town made famous by Samuel.

But we are not seeing the Gibeah of Saul. Instead here is a city that looks very much like Sodom. Centuries later the prophet Hosea wrote about the punishment of Israel and used this little insignificant city as an historical simile: "The things my people do are as depraved as what they did in Gibeah long ago. The Lord does not forget. He will surely punish them (Hos. 9:9, TLB). And again, "Oh Israel, ever since that awful night in Gibeah, there has been only sin, sin, sin! You have made no progress whatever. Was it not right that the men of Gibeah were wiped out?" (Hos. 10:9, TLB). These are not allusions to the hanging of Saul's descendants (2 Sam. 21:6) or the fleeing of the people of Gibeah when the Assyrians marched against them (Isa. 10:29), but rather a direct reference to the "Sodom of Judah" depicted here in Judges 19.

Comparison With Sodom

The likeness between Judges 19 and Genesis 19 goes far beyond the identical chapter numbers in their respective Old Testament books. There are at least five key points of comparison that made these two cities alike a target for the wrath of God.

1. *Both Sodom and Gibeah were inhospitable cities.* Considerable space was given in chapter two to a discussion of the passage in Ezekiel that pinpoints Sodom and Gomorrah as suffering from the sin of inhospitality. It is unclear to me exactly how that sin links itself with the basic immorality of these two cities, but apparently withdrawn and ingrown moral standards made such towns suspicious of outsiders. Indeed, the very Hebrew root from which the word

Sodom is taken has to do with the idea of secrecy.

Gibeah, likewise, was an inhospitable town. The wandering Levite complained to the old man, ". . . 'I live on the far edge of the Ephraim hill country, near Shiloh, but no one has taken us in for the night, even though we have fodder for our donkeys, and plenty of food and wine for ourselves' " (Judg. 19:18,19; TLB).

2. *The streets of both cities were unsafe.* It was unthinkable to the old man, who by this time had learned something of the city he was visiting, that these strangers should stay in the streets after dark. It was just plain dangerous. Here one is reminded, of course, of the major cities of North America in our day. Fear caused by the constant threat of sexual molestation, muggings, and general crime in the streets is apparently not an invention of the technological society. And it is interesting how sexual crimes have continued to be prominent in wicked cities over these hundreds of years.

3. *The primary sin of both cities was the practice of homosexuality.* Any denial of this simple fact can only be a result of premeditated prejudice. Robert Watson identified the sexual nature of the sin of Gibeah.

> The crime of Gibeah brought under our notice here connects itself with that of Sodom and represents a phase of immorality which, indigenous to Canaan, mixed its putrid current with Hebrew life. There are traces of the same horrible impurity in the Judah of Rehoboam and Asa; and in the story of Josiah's reign we are horrified to read of "houses of sodomites that were in the house of the Lord, where the women wove hangings for Asherah." With such lurid historical light on the subject, we can easily understand the revival of

this warning lesson from the past of Israel and the fullness of detail with which the incidents are recorded. A crime originally that of the offscourings of Gibeah became practically the sin of a whole tribe, and the warning that ensued sets in a clear light the zeal for domestic purity which was a feature in every religious revival and, at length, in the life of the Hebrew people.[2]

4. *The homosexuals in both cities used the technique of gang rape.* One can only assume that the way those in Judges 19 perpetrated their debauchery on the concubine represents their *modus operandi,* which would have also been used on the Levite himself. Like the Sodomites in Genesis 19:9, they surrounded the house and beat on the door. And like the Sodomites, they were also bisexuals who could vent their immoral propensities upon male or female alike, though obviously their preferences ran toward persons of their own sex.

This kind of passage should deliver us once and for all from the notion that homosexuals by and large are just a nice quiet group of people who want to be left alone to "do their own thing." Although many homosexuals fit this description, there is more to the picture. Hardly a week goes by that major newspapers do not record the account of some enforced seduction and even violent rape of a homosexual nature. Quite obviously, heterosexual rape is a far more widespread crime, and it is not the intent of this chapter to minimize it and maximize the heinousness of homosexual rape. Both are horrendous sins in the

[2]"Judges and Ruth," W. Robertson Nicoll, ed., *The Expositor's Bible,* vol. 7 (London: Hodder and Stoughton, 1889), pp. 348–49.

sight of God and one is not to be excused because of the existence or even the preponderance of the other!

5. *The so-called righteous men of both cities were willing to substitute women to avoid what they considered to be the worse crime of homosexual relations.* Lot was willing to send out his daughters, as was the old man of Judges 19. In actuality the Levite himself took the concubine and shoved her out of the house into the lecherous hands of the waiting mob. Charles Ellicott pointed up the very depths of depravity to which the nation had fallen that such a substitution should be even thought of, much less executed.

> But we must not omit to notice that the conduct of the old man and the Levite, though it is not formally condemned, speaks of the existence of a very rudimentary morality, a selfishness, and a low estimate of the rights and sacred dignity of women, which shows from what depths the world has emerged. If it was possible to frustrate the vile assault of these wretches in this way it must have been possible to frustrate it altogether. There is something terribly repulsive in the selfishness which could thus make a Levite sacrifice a defenseless woman, and that woman his wife, for a whole night to such brutalization.[3]

Exegesis of the Text

There are several words and phrases in the key verses of Judges 19 that must be explored in depth if our study is to be thorough. First of all, the phrase "sons of Belial" in verse 22 carries with it in most

---

[3]*A Bible Commentary for English Readers*, vol. 2 (London: Cassell and Company, Ltd., n.d.), p. 262.

texts an unfortunate capitalization of the main word. Actually *belial* is simply a transliteration of the Hebrew word for *worthlessness*. These were not men motivated by an evil spirit, but worthless fellows or good-for-nothings, the rabble of the town. The verb describing their knocking indicates a gradual increase in volume and intensity so that the safety of the house's inhabitants was increasingly in doubt.

Also in verse 22 we encounter again that Hebrew word used in the Sodom account, *yoda*. There is no need to rehash the arguments here since anyone willing to face the evidence of the use of this verb to indicate sexual activities within a given context must come to the conclusion that it is used in that sense here, as it was in the Sodom account of Genesis 19.

In verse 23 the word *folly* appears in the Authorized Version. The word is the Hebrew *nevoloh*, which carries with it the idea of worthlessness as opposed to other Hebrew words so translated that carry more the idea of vanity *(toheloh)*, absurdity *(tiphloh)*, and foolishness *(ivveleth)*. This is not the sole instance where *nevoloh* is connected with sexual immorality (see Gen. 34:7 and Deut. 22:21) though it is not always so used.

The danger here is to think that the Scripture is treating the act of the men of Gibeah lightly by using the word *folly*. F. W. Farrar, at one time the dean of Canterbury and the man who wrote the commentary on Judges in the Ellicott series, suggested a reason for the use:

It is from no deficiency of moral indignation that the word "folly" is used. Sometimes when crime is too dark and deadly for ordinary reproach, the feelings are more deeply expressed by using a

> milder word, which is instantly corrected and intensified by the hearer himself.[4]

So intended rape became actual rape and resulted in murder. The image of the abused concubine lying dead with her fingers frozen on the threshold is one of the dark pictures of Old Testament history. And the degeneracy of the times is only further complicated by the act of the Levite who, according to the text, "took a knife, and laid hold on his concubine, and divided her, together with her bones, into twelve pieces, and sent her into all the coasts of Israel" (Judg. 19:29). This was obviously a symbolic act, a grandstand play to set the crime of the city before the eyes of a whole nation in a way that could not be ignored.

What the Levite expected came to pass. The congregation of Israel assembled at Mizpah to sentence Gibeah and determined to punish the crime. In a startling turn of events, the Benjaminites refused to deliver up the offenders, organized to offer resistance, and were actually successful in warding off the attacks of the other tribes not once but twice! Again, the sovereignty of God is depicted in Judges 20. Though the men of Benjamin and Gibeah were definitely in the wrong, God used them to punish the other tribes first. He then turned His judgment against Gibeah by allowing it to be burned to the ground, and against Benjamin by allowing its army to be completely routed.

All the men and cattle found in any towns of the tribe were slain, and the towns were left in ashes so that the whole tribe of Benjamin was annihilated with the exception of a small remnant. The whole episode

[4]Ibid., p. 262.

allows the Book of Judges to end on a sorry note and everybody loses. But that's the way with sin, everybody always loses when it is allowed to run rampant in any city or nation. The national reaction to the crime may have been commendable, but the brashness of the act was not within the boundaries of good sense. Keil and Delitzsch expressed it this way:

> However just and laudable the moral indignation may have been, which was expressed in that oath by the nation generally at the scandalous crime of the Gibeites, a crime unparalleled in Israel, and at the favor shown to the culprits by the tribe of Benjamin, the oath itself was an act of rashness, in which there was not only an utter denial of brotherly love, but the bounds of justice were broken through. When the elders of the nation came to a better state of mind, they ought to have acknowledged their rashness openly, and freed themselves, and the nation from an oath that had been taken in such sinful haste.[5]

So there we have the tale of two cities, Sodom and Gibeah, sister cities in the sin of homosexuality and its accompanying disastrous results. In linking Gibeah with Sodom, the poet Milton offers these lines in *Paradise Lost:*

> And when night darkens the streets,
>   Then wander forth the sons of Belial,
> Full of innocence and wine.

> Witness the streets of Sodom and that night,
>   In Gibeah, when the hospitable door
> Exposed a matron to avoid worse rape.

---

[5]"Joshua, Judges, Ruth," *Biblical Commentary on the Old Testament,* reprint ed. (Grand Rapids: Eerdmans, 1950), p. 464.

It was definitely the worst of times, not the best of times. Anarchy, as a system of government, was not working, even though its excessive corruption of human government and relations was lifted from time to time by the appearance of a God-appointed judge. The simple fact is that the theocracy, a nation controlled from heaven by the God of creation, had been abandoned in the lives and behavior of the Israeli nation, and they apparently had no intention of turning back to it even under the godly leadership of Samuel, the prophet-priest.

Their next act was to take a king like the other nations, and so our next task is to see how the ancient Hebrews fared in a monarchial system with respect to the serious commitment of the nation and its leaders to morality in sexual behavior.

CHAPTER 5

THEIRS WAS NOT THE KINGDOM

Just as homosexuality made its appearance during the time of the judges, in those periods when no judge or perhaps a weak judge was in control, so during the time of the monarchy were the sodomites found to be active or underground depending on the spiritual quality of the king. The Hebrew word *qadesh* appears six times in the Old Testament. One time it is translated "unclean" in the Authorized Version text of Job 36:14. The other five times it is translated by the word "sodomite." Of those five instances four are in the two books of Kings (the other is in Deut. 23:7, which we studied in a previous chapter).

Two eras of history are visited upon Israel between Judges 19 and the beginning of the monarchy. The first is the period of the judges itself, beginning with the rise of Othniel about 1390 B.C. and ending with the emergence of Samuel in about 1050 B.C. Then the tribe of Benjamin burst back into the news, this time with a "good press," as Samuel was sent to anoint Saul about 1043 B.C. There is actually an overlap of the period of the judges well into Samuel's ministry as prophet and priest. Samson may possibly have begun judging two years before Eli's death. Continuing for twenty years, he was almost a contemporary of Samuel (who may have begun his judgeship as early as 1067 B.C.) who, in turn, overlapped Saul until the death of the prophet in 1020 B.C. The dates are approximate and in any event not the focus of our concern in this chapter. The point is that Gibeah had lived down the nightmare we studied earlier so that we can read in 1 Samuel 10:26, "And Saul also went home to Gibeah; and there went with him a band of men, whose hearts God had touched."

Rehoboam

For approximately one hundred and twenty years there is no mention of sodomites in Israel. Each of the three kings in the united kingdom reigned for forty years so that the books of 1 and 2 Samuel and half of 1 Kings do not mention the *qadesh* in Israel, though one may very well suppose it was still an underground movement of the unclean who were afraid to surface because of the control Saul, David, and Solomon had on civic and social affairs.

Enter Rehoboam, who after the death of his father Solomon called for a national assembly at Shechem. Jeroboam returned from Egypt where he had fled after displeasing Solomon with his talk of revolution. Keep in mind that the prophet Ahijah had already dramatically communicated God's choice of Jeroboam to rule ten tribes by ripping his mantle into twelve pieces and handing Jeroboam ten of the pieces.

At the Shechem summit, Rehoboam announced even higher taxes, an act that prompted Jeroboam to lead ten seceding tribes, leaving Judah and Benjamin alone supporting Rehoboam. The kingdom was divided forever. Jeroboam hardly became a godly king in the North, but it was Rehoboam who corrupted Jerusalem with his ungodliness. Of his reign we read:

> And Judah did evil in the sight of the LORD, and they provoked Him to jealousy more than all that their fathers had done, with the sins which they committed. For they also built for themselves high places and sacred pillars and Asherim on every high hill and beneath every luxuriant tree. And there were also male cult prostitutes in the land. They did according to all the abominations of the nations which the LORD dispossessed before the sons of Israel (1 Kings 14:22-24, NASB).

Why did he do it? Why did Rehoboam reintroduce the ungodliness so frequently condemned in the Mosaic Law? Without minimizing his own corruption, we surely must understand that part of Rehoboam's problem must be charged to his father Solomon. The wisest man who ever lived became himself deeply mired in apostasy and idolatry before his death (1 Kings 11:9-13), but for David's sake, judgment was postponed until after the death of his son. Part of Rehoboam's legacy was a debt for the sins of his father.

But Rehoboam's mother had not been much help either. In the typical pattern, Naamah, an Ammonitess, had become one of Solomon's multiple queens and had no doubt distorted the early religious education of her son until his tolerance of sodomy corrupted the nation when he became king. Samuel Schultz described Rehoboam's reign in a terse paragraph.

> In spite of his initial religious fervor Rehoboam succumbed to idolatry. Iddo, the prophet who wrote a history of Rehoboam's reign, may have

been God's messenger to advise the king. In addition to increased idolatry and invasions by Egypt, intermittent warfare between the North and the South made the days of Rehoboam times of turmoil. The Southern Kingdom declined rapidly under his leadership.[1]

The incomplete destruction of the Canaanites haunted Israel all the years it was in the land. And along with idolatry came homosexuality. Together they became a religious and social epidemic during the divided monarchy.

In a brief three-year reign, Rehoboam's son Abijah carried out the evil policies of his father by continuing religious pluralism. He didn't abolish the temple worship of Jehovah, but he did simultaneously condone the worship of foreign gods. The only thing that protected the nation from a complete overthrow of the Solomonic line was God's covenantal promise to David (1 Kings 15:4,5).

Asa

The young King Asa instituted a reform that resulted in a removal of the sodomites from the land (1 Kings 15:12). He broke down foreign altars and high places of worship and destroyed the pollutions of the Asherim. The Mosaic Law became again a matter of great concern in the land and the result was a God-given peace for about fourteen years after the death of Abijah. Unfortunately, Asa did not end his monarchial career as positively as he had begun it. He reigned for forty-one years but only the first fifteen were marked by godliness.

[1]*The Old Testament Speaks* (New York: Harper & Row, 1960), p. 184.

The association of idolatry with sodomy is revealed in an interesting manner during the monarchial period. The verse quoted above (1 Kings 15:12) shows how closely the two are aligned in the thinking of God. Asa was commended for doing "that which was right in the eyes of the Lord, as did David his father" (15:13). What was right in the eyes of God? Apparently to (1) kick the sodomites out of the land, and (2) remove all the idols. Natural depravity and spiritual depravity go hand in hand.

Jehoshaphat

Even though some of the sodomites escaped the reform attempts of Asa, they were caught in the revivals that came in under the leadership of Jehoshaphat (872–848 B.C.). The story of this godly king is told primarily in 2 Chronicles, but the last chapter of 1 Kings describes his reforms in Judah.

> And he walked in all the way of Asa his father; he did not turn aside from it, doing right in the sight of the LORD. However, the high places were not taken away; the people still sacrificed and burnt incense on the high places. Jehoshaphat also made peace with the king of Israel. Now the rest of the acts of Jehoshaphat, and his might which he showed and how he warred, are they not written in the Book of the Chronicles of the Kings of Judah? And the remnant of the sodomites who remained in the days of his father Asa, he expelled from the land (1 Kings 22:43-46, NASB).

It is of great significance that the Scripture frequently reports the cutting off of the sodomites by the good kings. Alfred Barry spells out the dynamic of the *qadesh* concept.

There is a horrible significance in the derivation of this word, which is properly "consecrated," or "devoted"; for it indicates the license, and even the sanction, of unnatural lusts in those consecrated to the abominations of Nature-worship. The appearance of such in the land, whether Canaanites or apostate Israelites, is evidently noted as the climax of the infinite corruption which had set in, rivaling—and, if rivaling, exceeding in depth of wickedness—the abominations of the old inhabitants of the land.

That such horrors are not incompatible with advance in knowledge and material civilization, history tells us but too plainly. To find them sanctioned under cover of religious ritual marks, however, a lower depth still.[2]

In the post-Solomonic kingdom, we would have expected to find an enlightened people. It was one thing to practice homosexuality in the days of Gibeah, a period of darkness in the nation between the death of Joshua and the reforms of some of the judges. It is quite another thing to have experienced one hundred and twenty years of the united kingdom under the obvious blessing of Jehovah and then to turn back again to the abominations of the Canaanites.

Likewise, it is a shame for the people of North America who have experienced such obvious blessing from God to turn their backs upon that God, upon His laws, upon His moral code, and not only tolerate sodomy in the land, but to actually make laws to nurture and advance its abominations. The freedoms of democracy are no longer freedoms when they are

[2]Ellicott, *Bible Commentary for English Readers*, pp. 69–70.

contemptuous of the biblical morality upon which any lasting government must be founded. To be sure, morality cannot be legislated, but on the other hand, there is no need to legislate immorality!

Josiah

But our study of homosexuality during the monarchy ends on a high note with the reforms of the good king Josiah. As we look in on him in 2 Kings, the year is 621 B.C. and Hilkiah, the high priest, has recently discovered the book of the Law in the house of the Lord, which had been repaired by the king's command. Having read the book, the king orders reforms similar to those ordered by Asa and Jehoshaphat.

Then the king commanded Hilkiah the high priest and the priests of the second order and the doorkeepers, to bring out of the temple of the LORD all the vessels that were made for Baal, for Asherah, and for all the host of heaven; and he burned them outside Jerusalem in the fields of the Kidron, and carried their ashes to Bethel. And he did away with the idolatrous priests whom the kings of Judah had appointed to burn incense in the high places in the cities of Judah and in the surrounding area of Jerusalem, also those who burned incense to Baal, to the sun and to the moon and to the constellations and to all the host of heaven. And he brought out the Asherah from the house of the LORD outside Jerusalem to the brook Kidron, and burned it at the brook Kidron, and ground it to dust, and threw its dust on the graves of the common people. He also broke down the houses of the male cult prostitutes which were in the house of the LORD, where the women were weaving hangings for the Asherah.

> Then he brought all the priests from the cities of Judah, and defiled the high places where the priests had burned incense, from Geba to Beersheba; and he broke down the high places of the gates which were at the entrance of the gate of Joshua the governor of the city, which were on one's left at the city gate (2 Kings 23:4-8, NASB).

The Northern Kingdom had already gone into captivity (722 B.C.) and world power was in the process of being transferred from Assyria to Babylonia. The Assyrians would fall to the Medes in 614 B.C., and Babylonia would be in control of the world before the turn of the century. But this was a time of peace and righteous reforms under young Josiah who became king at the age of eight and lived only thirty-nine years. A new phrase is added to the destruction of the sodomites (v. 7) as we read about women who wove "hangings for the Asherah." This is a reference to the fact that women actually decorated worship trappings for Asherah in the temple at Jerusalem. These fancy accoutrements were a part of the pagan chambers of cult prostitution connected with the worship of false gods. As late as 592 B.C., Ezekiel prophesied God's judgment against Jerusalem's unfaithfulness.

> "Then your fame went forth among the nations on account of your beauty, for it was perfect because of My splendor which I bestowed on you," declares the Lord GOD. "But you trusted in your beauty and played the harlot because of your fame, and you poured out your harlotries on every passer-by who might be willing. And you took some of your clothes, made for yourself high places of various colors, and played the harlot on them, which should never come about nor happen. You also took your beautiful jewels

made of My gold and of My silver, which I had
given you, and made for yourself male images
that you might play the harlot with them. Then
you took your embroidered cloth and covered
them, and offered My oil and My incense before
them" (Ezek. 16:14-18, NASB).

A most horrid idolatry had prevailed for over half a
century before Josiah. Manasseh and Amon had
plunged themselves into the support of paganism
even to the point of persecuting the true worshippers
of Jehovah. Unfortunately the revival under Josiah
may have only been a surface experience that affected the common people very little. Abominations
were restrained as long as Josiah lived, but immediately after his death the people reverted to the
same idolatry and wickedness under Jehoiakim. That
is why Jeremiah, who began his prophetic ministry in
the thirteenth year of Josiah's reign, reflected the
strained relationship between God and Israel with
the analogy of the faithless wife who breaks her marriage vows.

It is important to note that all four of the kings we
have studied in this chapter were kings of the Southern Kingdom, that is they were in the line of the more
righteous kings. God alone knows the abominations
that went on up north among the ten tribes before
their capture by Assyria in 722 B.C. It is a depressing
story in which some of the northern kings are depicted as being more depraved than the residents of
pagan nations around them! Nineteen kings ruled in
Israel culminating with Hoshea. Twenty kings ruled
in Judah. Eight of them received good marks from
God, and their collective rule extended more than
twice as many years as the twelve evil kings.

There are great lessons to be learned from what we

too frequently consider a dull portion of the Bible, namely, the history of Israel. "Righteousness exalteth a nation: but sin is a reproach to any people" (Prov. 14:34), and that is only too evident from the history of the monarchy. To be sure, we do not live in a theocracy today and things are a great deal different in many respects. But the law of sin and retribution is surely still a principle of God's control in His world, and He will surely exercise His right of condemnation upon a sinful people in due time. And if we read Scripture correctly, one of the national sins that disgraces a nation and makes it a stench in the nostrils of a Holy God is the activity of sodomites in the land.

From the end of the monarchy to the beginning of the New Testament some four hundred years passed, often called the "four hundred silent years." But God was there and He was not silent. He was working in human history through pagan nations like the Babylonians, the Chaldeans, the Medes, the Persians, the Greeks, and eventually the Romans, who were in control when the star led the wise men to the Holy Land.

CHAPTER 6

BLAME IT ON THE GREEKS!

The Romans with their thundering legions tromping over almost every inch of the Mediterranean world before, during, and after the time of Christ were at first appearance completely different from their predecessors in world dominion, the Greeks. Yet the culture, language, and impact of the Greeks lingered on as evidenced by the writing of the New Testament in Greek during the time of Rome's greatest authority.

Greek society had been very lax with respect to homosexuality. "Free love" was virtually unknown in Greece between a man and a woman, since payment in such a relationship was assumed, but love affairs with *ephebi* (young men) were quite common and pederasty ran rampant throughout Greek society. William Cole has written:

> Homosexuality was common, as it still is today, all over the region of the Eastern Mediterranean far more than in the West. But the Greeks had a special taste for it. No physiological differences are apparent as explanatory of this phenomenon, and the cause must be sought in the environment. The ideal of beauty as the slim, boyish figure

probably had much to do with it, as Lewinsohn suggests. . . . The existence of such accepted relationships in the society made in itself for a certain predisposition. . . . The first sexual experiences are strongly determinative of future attitudes and practices. Boys early seduced by older men, appealing alike to curiosity and prurience, to vanity and greed, were not averse to continuing such relationships, especially where no social censure accompanied these pleasures.[1]

Homosexuality among the Greeks was primarily a male phenomenon, but hardly uniquely so. It is from the famous Sappho who ran a school for girls on the isle of Lesbos that we get the term *lesbianism,* usually used to describe sexual relationships between women.

Then came the Romans whose infatuation with heterosexuality and detestation of the effeminate Greeks created a society in which homosexuality was certainly present but did not achieve dominance as it had among the worshippers of Mount Olympus. The Romans were guilty of all kinds of insidious immorality, one of the most common of which was prostitution, but they were not *pedophiles* like the Greeks. The early Christians who came out of gentile backgrounds knew very well the immorality of both cultures and regarded Rome as "the whore of Babylon" and a fitting model for the perversity of an entire pagan society.

Derrick Bailey blames the Christian attitude toward homosexuality on what he calls a "reinterpretation of the Sodom story," an error, according to Bailey, in which even the apostle Paul was caught

---

[1]*Sex and Love in the Bible* (New York: Association Press 1959), pp. 202–03.

up—as we shall see in a moment. Bailey openly admits:

> Both the Bible and the Roman law encouraged a severe treatment of sodomy, but there was also a mitigating influence, partly theological and partly ecclesiastical in character, which has usually been overlooked. Justinian, in his edicts, had insisted that homosexual acts were sins as well as crimes, and that the penalties of the secular law were only to be invoked against the obdurate and the unrepentant—and there is a strange irony in the fact that the emperor who sought to temper judgment with mercy has often been blamed for inculcating an attitude which derives chiefly from the harsher rigor of the Theodosian Code.[2]

It is precisely these influences, which are "partly theological and partly ecclesiastical in character," that have made necessary the early paragraphs of this chapter describing the contrast between the Greeks and the Romans. Bailey's whole case stands or falls on whether homosexuality was the sin for which Sodom was destroyed. He argues vehemently that it was *not* and claims that the early Christians, presumably including the apostle Paul, were only attacking homosexuality because of the abhorrence they had for its dominance in Greek society. Be aware that a full treatment of Bailey's thesis appears in Appendix 1 of this book, but we must reproduce here a rather lengthy demonstration of his incredible conclusion regarding New Testament understandings of the Sodom account.

Nevertheless, our investigation shows that there

[2]*Homosexuality and the Western Christian Tradition* (Hamden, Conn.: Archon Books, 1975), p. 158.

is not the least reason to believe, as a matter either of historical fact or of revealed truth, that the city of Sodom and its neighbours were destroyed because of their homosexual practices. This theory of their fate seems undoubtedly to have originated in a Palestinian Jewish reinterpretation of Gen. xix, inspired by antagonism to the Helenistic way of life and its exponents and by contempt for the basest features of Greek sexual immorality.

From this part of our inquiry, therefore, we may conclude that the Sodom story has no direct bear ing whatever upon the problem of homosexuality or the commission of homosexual acts. Hence it is no longer possible to maintain the belief that homosexual practices were once punished by a Divine judgment upon their perpetrators so terri ble and conclusive as to preclude any subsequent discussion of the question. Still less can it be held that an act of God has determined once for all what attitude Church and State ought to adopt toward the problem of sexual inversion. This is not to say that homosexual acts may not, in a greater or lesser degree, be sinful; but only that their morality falls to be decided (like that of other human acts) by reference to the natural law, and in accordance with the principles of Christian ethics and moral theology, and cannot be considered settled by a natural catastrophe which occurred in the remote past.[3]

So in one fell swoop Bailey concludes that the Sodom and Gomorrah account was a "natural catastrophe" rather than divine intervention; that the biblical account of the city of Sodom has no bearing on New Testament understandings of homosexuality;

[3]Ibid., pp. 27–28.

that the apostle Paul and other New Testament writers held distorted views of homosexuality because of Helenistic influences; and that we can, in short, blame it all on the Greeks!

Biblical Exegesis

But I am *most* interested in what Bailey is willing to grant, namely that homosexual acts may indeed be sinful, and that their morality must be decided by an appeal to the natural law and the principles of Christian ethics and moral theology. So here's the question: Is the natural law properly understood by evangelicals, and are the principles of Christian ethics and moral theology linked with Old Testament history? And what precisely does Paul mean in his condemnation of the Greeks, the Romans, and all other barbarian societies in Romans 1:18-32?

Before looking at the key verses (24-27), it is important to see the entire flow of the first chapter of Romans. James Stiflar sees the chapter as a broad survey of paganism in general with a specific attempt to show how the gospel is suited to every moral and national condition. After a brief salutation in the first seven verses, Paul greeted the brethren in verses 8 through 17. Then in the major theological thrust of the chapter he pronounced the guilt of the gentile world throughout all times and in all places.[4] Paul pronounced God's divine retribution against those who had violated both *natural law* and *natural revelation*.

As exegetes have learned, in Paul's writings there is generally a clue to the structure of his theology,

[4]James Stiflar, *The Epistle to the Romans* (Chicago: Moody Press, 1974), p. 23.

and in Romans 1:24-28 the divine judgment is accen
tuated by the threefold use of the Greek word
paredoken (to give over).

> Therefore *God gave them over* in the sinful de-
> sires of their hearts to sexual impurity for the
> degrading of their bodies with one another. They
> exchanged the truth of God for a lie, and wor-
> shipped and served created things rather than the
> Creator—who is forever praised. Amen. Be-
> cause of this, *God gave them over* to shameful
> lusts. Even their women exchanged natural rela-
> tions for unnatural ones. In the same way the
> men also abandoned natural relations with
> women and were inflamed with lust for one
> another. Men committed indecent acts with
> other men, and received in themselves the due
> penalty for their perversion. Furthermore, since
> they did not think it worthwhile to retain the
> knowledge of God, *he gave them over* to a de-
> praved mind, to do what ought not to be done
> (Rom. 1:24-28, NIV, italics added).

Burl Delong's research indicates that three con-
tending viewpoints clamor for acceptance regarding
the meaning of *paredoken* as it is used in this crucial
passage. Some define the term in a permissive sense;
that is, God allowed men to have their own sinful
way. Others emphasize a privative sense suggesting
that God withdrew from man His common grace or
aid. In *Bibliotheca Sacra,* however, S. Lewis
Johnson suggests a much stronger impact of the word
indicating that the phrase "God gave them up" describes a judicial act. God did not just withdraw the
restraining force of good, but actually gave men over
to judgment because of their behavior.

This interpretation is also in harmony with the occurrence of the precisely identical form in Acts 7:42, where, in speaking of Israel's apostasy in the days of Moses, Stephen says, "Then God turned, and gave them up (Gr., *paredoken*) to worship the host of heaven." Both the Romans and the Acts passages describe the act of God as a penal infliction of retribution, the expression of an essential attribute of God's nature and being and it is thoroughly consistent with His holiness.[5]

A common gay approach to the harsh language of Romans 1 is to fall back on what has become known as "the abuse argument." The view seeks to justify homosexual behavior by arguing that the New Testament speaks against homosexual *abuse* but not against *"responsible" homosexual behavior*. Kim Stablinksi has stated it simply.

Note these key words: change, leaving. In order to change from or to leave heterosexuality, one must first be heterosexual.

What we have is an account of bisexual lust—and St. Paul does say lust, placing this behavior out of the higher realm of love and devotion.[6]

What we are looking at, of course, is the violation of the biblical norm, namely heterosexuality. This is the point of Romans 1:26 and 27, that the natural

[5]"God Gave Them Up," *Bibliotheca Sacra* (April-June 1972): 127–28.
[6]"Homosexuality, What the Bible Does and Does not Say," *The Ladder* (July 1969).

sexual proclivity of man is not for other men, but for women (Gen. 2:18-25). Application of the abuse principle in this context misses the whole issue of natural law and design, and fails to recognize that all biblical passages that deal with homosexuality are concerned with specific prohibition of such behavior, which in itself is the abuse. There is not legitimate and illegitimate adultery—all adultery is sin. There is not legitimate or illegitimate idolatry—all idolatry is sin. And by the same token, there is not legitimate homosexuality and illegitimate homosexuality—all homosexuality is illicit behavior according to biblical norms in both natural and special revelation.

In the reference cited above, Stablinski wants us to believe that gay Christians have never turned from a natural heterosexual condition to an unnatural homosexual one, and it would be unnatural for them to become heterosexual. But this assumes a scientifically unwarranted argument that the homosexual was born in that condition.

Ralph Blair further confuses the interpretation of the passage by playing word games and referring to the pagan behavior of homosexuality as an "unfortunate structural problem."

> In the latter, the practice is seen as a resultant and unfortunate structural problem in the world after the Fall from the original created order. Others of these evidences which Paul mentions are disobedience to parents, envy, and gossip. The homosexual reference, however, seems literally most fitting since it illustrates what was perceived to be a reversal of a norm variously described by Paul as the exchange of the truth for a lie, professing wisdom for foolishness, and

honoring and serving the creature more than the
Creator.[7]

Blair simply refuses to recognize that the Bible
does not allow for "good homosexuals" and "bad
homosexuals." Depravity is depravity and perversion is perversion—Paul had no time for semantic
games. Blair also wants us to believe that Paul simply
used homosexuality as an illustration of the depravity of the Roman culture while the behavior itself was
not depraved. And here his sometimes cogent argument turns to nonsense. How can an illustration of
depravity not be depravity itself? Klaus Bockmühl
dashes the fragile case to bits on the rock-bound
coast of clear thinking.

> If the whole pattern is rejected as depraved, how
> can we accept the feature of it that is expressly
> cited as an illustration? Others claim that
> homosexuality is presented not as sinful in itself,
> but is punishment for sin. This explanation is
> more than naive. In Romans 1, Paul is completely
> in tune with the Old Testament idea that God can
> punish a sin by delivering the sinner over to it
> completely.[8]

As DeLong tells us, beginning in Genesis and
throughout the entire revelation of Scripture, the
natural sexual function is described as the male–
female relationship. Proverbs 5:18,19 commend a
man to be sexually satisfied with a woman. First
Corinthians 7:2 states that to prevent immorality a
man is to unite himself sexually with a wife and a

[7]Blair, "Evangelical Look at Homosexuality": 7.

[8]"Homosexuality and Biblical Perspective," *Christianity
Today* (16 February 1973): 14.

woman with a husband. It is logically unsound and exegetically preposterous to believe that Romans 1:26,27 assume a "natural" homosexuality that originates from the creative hand of God. *Homosexual behavior originates from the depravity of man.*

Practical Application

So God has condemned homosexuality in Greece, in Rome, and in every society, from the barbarian Sodom to the sophisticated Western cultures of the late twentieth century. And situational arguments about motives, or word games about what is natural and what is unnatural, cannot change the clear meaning of Romans 1 for the evangelical Christian Homosexuality, particularly in the blatant gay activism of our day, is a contemporary demonstration of Paul's description of men who had "abandoned natural relations with women and were inflamed with lust for one another. Men committed indecent acts with other men, and received in themselves the due penalty for their perversion" (Rom. 1:27, NIV).

God always suits the punishment to the crime, or more particularly, to the sin. Everett F. Harrison tells us how clearly God designs a society's judgment to fit its perversions.

> Sexual deviation contains in itself a recompense, a punishment for the abandonment of God and His ways. This need not demand the conclusion that every homosexual follows the practice in deliberate rebellion against God's prescribed order. What is true historically and theologically is in measure true, however, experientially. The "gay" facade is a thin veil for a deep-seated

frustration. The folly of homosexuality is proclaimed in its inability to reproduce the human species in keeping with the divine commandment (Genesis 1:28). To sum up, what men do with God has much to do with their character and life style.[9]

So we must thank Bailey (quoted earlier) for calling us back to a concern for natural law and natural revelation. That is precisely what Paul was talking about in Romans 1. The natural function of which the apostle spoke was clearly that designed by God as described in the Book of Genesis, and the unnatural function was man's design, a perversion resulting from a distorted theology that brings God down to man's level and worships the creature more than the Creator.

God gave them up. But when did this judicial act of the Creator take place? Paul's emphasis on the Genesis passage would seem to indicate that it was a part of retribution for the Fall. When men rebelled against the truth of God as revealed to them, God turned them over to their own lusts, which were born of Satan himself. The judicial declaration was a part of the judgment of the Fall, though the actual experience takes place in the course of a person's life as he turns against God's truth to the point where he too is given up.

Of course, since we have no idea what that point is in God's perfect plan, the repentant homosexual is accepted and forgiven in the same way as a repentant person who has been guilty of any other sin—any violation of God's natural law and moral principles.

[9]"Romans," Frank E. Gaebelein, ed., *The Expositor's Bible Commentary* (Grand Rapids: Zondervan, 1976), p. 25.

Paul's argument is that such repentance will be the exception rather than the norm in a barbarian society—and we cannot just blame it on the Greeks!

The only ultimate solution for homosexuality is described in 2 Corinthians 5:17 where the apostle tells us that the old things are passed away and all things become new when Christ changes not only the "heart," but also the life-style of the repentant sinner.

CHAPTER 7

SUCH WERE SOME OF YOU

Jim Carlson is an alcoholic. He wasn't born that way. There was nothing in the make-up of his genes or the behavior of his parents that caused his alcoholism; in fact, he never had a drink until he was an adult. But after his initial exposure to alcohol, Jim became a practicing alcoholic and fell completely under the control of that insidious drug.

At what point in Jim's experience was sin the cause of alcoholism and at what point was alcoholism the cause of sin? Or to put it another way, what is the difference between sin and sickness in the case of alcoholism? These questions are very difficult to answer, but one thing is clear: God has the desire as well as the power to deliver Jim from alcoholism if he will come to the point of recognizing its destructive tendencies as well as its violation of God's laws and will allow himself to be changed by divine power through either natural or supernatural means.

Homosexuality is much like this illustration except that the analogy does not follow through on two or three crucial points. Most evangelicals would not suggest that the Bible condemns an occasional drink, but they would agree that the Bible always condemns homosexual acts. By the same token, it is hardly possible to be an alcoholic without practicing a somewhat regular use of alcoholic beverages, but it is possible to have homosexual tendencies without engaging in homosexual practices. It is the *practice* and not the *propensity* that the Scripture condemns, but the practice can be forgiven and the propensity can be changed by the power of Jesus Christ. That is why we say the gospel is for the gay.

It is possible to have concluded by this time that I am attempting to portray homosexuality as something of an outstanding sin, perhaps just a bit more immoral than other kinds of sins that come out of paganism. If that idea has been conveyed, I want to disclaim it at this point. Homosexuality is one of many kinds of behavior that are characteristic of the pagan life-style our Lord died to change. This was essentially the message of Paul to the Corinthians, some of whom had been practicing homosexuals before the gospel of the Cross changed their lives.

> Don't you know that the wicked will not inherit the kingdom of God? Do not be deceived: Neither the sexually immoral nor idolaters nor adulterers nor male prostitutes nor homosexual offenders nor theives nor the greedy nor drunkards nor slanderers nor swindlers will inherit the kingdom of God. And that is what some of you were. But you were washed, you were sanctified, you were justified in the name of the Lord Jesus Christ and by the Spirit of our God. (1 Cor. 6:9-11, NIV).

Homosexuality is a sin for which forgiveness is offered in Scripture. The problem is that if we believe that the apostle Paul and other New Testament writers were confused regarding the attitude of God toward homosexuality, we will be unable to call practicing homosexuals to repentance. A particular sin must be recognized as sin, not as a sin worse than any other type of ungodly behavior, but at least as sin that must be forsaken and for which redemption and renewal in Christ are possible. Excuses will never achieve the regeneration God offers. John White writes:

> *Homosexual* is a morally loaded term. It should be confined to those who engage in homosexual acts. The people we label may have neither the wish nor even the impulse to engage in such acts, and we have no right to besmirch them. On the other hand we must grasp that homosexual behavior is not in any sense inevitable in someone who engages in it. It may be understandable. But no homosexual (certainly no Christian homosexual) has the right to say, ''I am not responsible for what I do because my homosexual nature *makes me* do it.''[1]

Two Important Greek Words

First Corinthians 6:9 contains two Greek terms that are important to our understanding of homosexuality and God's offer of grace. The first is *malakoi,* which basically means ''soft'' or ''weak.'' The word has no particular moral connotation since it is often used in classical Greek literature to mean being effeminate as well as to describe morally loose behavior. It may very well have related to the Greek practice of pederasty. The word was sometimes used to

[1]*Eros Defiled* (Downers Grove, Ill.: InterVarsity Press, 1977), p. 111.

refer to men and boys who allowed themselves to be used homosexually.[2]

The second word is *arsenokoitai,* which appears both in 1 Corinthians 6:9 and 1 Timothy 1:10. (Unfortunately the *New International Version* translators chose to render the same word as "homosexual offenders" in 1 Corinthians and "perverts" in 1 Timothy. Presumably either translation is possible, but consistency would have been helpful.) *Arsenokoitai* comes from two words that when separated mean male *(arsen)* and coitus *(koita).* Arndt and Gingrich are probably quite accurate in translating *arsenokoitai* as "male homosexuals."

It is possible to define the *malakoi* as passive homosexuals, morally loose or effeminate persons who allow themselves to be used homosexually, and the *arsenokoitai* as active gays who aggressively pursue homosexual behavior.

Isn't it interesting that both sins are listed side by side with seemingly equal weight along with the other violations of both passages? And speaking of both passages, it might be useful here to reproduce the NIV rendering of 1 Timothy 1:9,10.

> We also know that the law is made not for good men, but for lawbreakers and rebels, the ungodly and sinful, the unholy and irreligious; for those who kill their fathers or mothers, for murderers, for adulterers and perverts, for slave traders and liars and perjurers—and for whatever else is contrary to the sound doctrine that conforms to the glorious gospel of the blessed God, which he entrusted to me.

[2]William F. Arndt and Wilbur Gingrich, trans., *A Greek-English Lexicon of the New Testament and Other Early Christian Literature,* 4th rev. ed. (Chicago: Univ. of Chicago Press, 1957), p. 489.

A great deal hinges on the proper translation of these Greek words, and although Derrick Bailey spends little time in the New Testament passages since he feels the New Testament writers were so obviously influenced in their thinking by the Hellenistic interpretations of the Sodom account, he does point up the importance of these words.

In 1 Cor. vi. 9 the technical words *malakoi* and *arsenokoitai* which denote respectively those males who engage passively or actively in homosexual acts, pose a problem which translators have not always happily solved. In the Authorized and Revised Versions "effeminate" hardly conveys the precise sense of *malakoi* to the modern reader, while "abusers of themselves with mankind," though not inadequate, is somewhat vague in that it could stand as a rendering of either *malakoi* or *arsenokoitai,* and would be better if it were not preceded by "effeminate. . . . But the translation approved by those responsible for the American Revised Standard Version is unfortunately both inaccurate and objectionable. In this revision, *malakoi* and *arsenokoitai* are represented by the single term "homosexuals"; and although a footnote draws attention to the fact that this expression stands for two Greek words, the words themselves are not mentioned, their meaning is not explained, and in particular it is not made clear that they apply solely to males who engage in homosexual acts. Above all, it is most regrettable that the revisers should have shown themselves unaware or unappreciative of the clear distinction which must be made between the homosexual *condition* (which is morally neutral) and homosexual *practices.* Use of the word "homosexuals" inevitably suggests that the genuine invert, even though he be a man of irreproachable morals, is automatically branded as unrighteous and excluded from the kingdom of God, just as if he were the most depraved of sexual perverts. Unless this error is corrected, and the true meaning of the passage is explained, the wide circulation of this version and the reputation which its general merit has won for it may only serve to encourage intolerance and to perpetuate a great social injustice, thus seriously discrediting the Christian Church.[3]

Bailey does not want the term "homosexuals" to appear in the text at all, arguing that the *malakoi* and *arsenokoitai* were not necessarily inverts but probably just "dissolute heterosexuals." He prefers Moffat's translation in 1913 that uses simply the terms "catamites and sodomites." This returns us to the old argument of good homosexuals and bad homosexuals.

We are quite willing to yield Bailey's point that there is a world of difference between homosexual propensity and practice; indeed that is one of the major theses of this volume. But it cannot be denied that the power of God, while offered in judgment against practicing homosexuals, stands ready to forgive and change those involved at the levels of both propensity and practice.

Exposition of the Passages

The first eleven verses of 1 Corinthians 6 concern Christian morality in legal matters. Apparently there was a practice among the Corinthians of settling

[3]Bailey, *Homosexuality and the Western Christian Tradition,* pp. 38–39.

property cases before non-Christian judges in Roman law courts. Paul argued that there was a higher ethic than Roman law—the divine standards a Christian community ought to apply in deciding such cases on its own. Indeed, the very existence of legal problems among believers shows malicious attitudes and spiritual immaturity.

This apparently led the apostle in his thinking to the stark contrast between those who have been regenerated and those who have not, and he concluded the section by reminding the Corinthians that practicing acts of wickedness *(adikeo)* was a life-style that prohibited entrance into the kingdom of God. W. Harold Mare points out that they simply were not thinking clearly about the meaning of holiness in the Christian life or about the drastic change that regeneration is to produce in the people of God.

> They are in a dangerous frame of mind—they need to clear their heads and realize that if they act wickedly in this way, they are no better than the wicked idolaters and others who will not inherit heaven. To the list of sinners already mentioned in 5:10,11, Paul points out specific kinds of sexually immoral people: the adulterers *(moichoi),* the male prostitutes *(malakoi)* and homosexuals *(arsenokoitai).* (In Romans 1:26 Paul also mentions lesbians.) Also added to his list here are those who are thieves *(kleptai).* In the light of this comparison, the Corinthians should have seen how unChristian and sinful their actions were toward one another.[4]

The use of *tauta* at the beginning of verse eleven is

[4]"1 Corinthians," Gaebelein, *Expositor's Bible Commentary,* pp. 222–23.

a startling appearance of the neuter gender—"some of you were these *things*." Is this a deliberate attempt on the part of the apostle and the Holy Spirit to emphasize the horrible condition of these pagan Corinthians before their salvation? If so, it is important to note that homosexuality is no worse than thievery, greediness, drunkenness, slander, idolatry, swindling, or general immorality.

May I say it again? The evangelical position on homosexuality is not that it is a worse sin than any other sin, but that *it is a sin* and therefore carries with it both condemnation and the possibility of forgiveness. God's grace reaches out in deep compassion to the repentant homosexual who recognizes his sin and wants to be changed. It is the militant gay who wishes to force his life-style on others as well as to require contemporary society to recognize its legitimacy who stands most in danger of God's open condemnation. Again, White's comment is helpful.

> Moreover it is not the sin itself which seems to awaken the wrath of God or of men of God in the Old and New Testaments. Rather it is the defiant attitude of glorying in their shame (an attitude which characterizes many homosexuals) which calls forth Divine indignation. The laughing demands of the lusters of Sodom and of the men in Judges 19 finds it parallel in the Greco-Roman civilization of Paul's day and in the gay movement leaders of today. It is this defiance of the divine order which is so offensive.[5]

The appearance of *arsenokoitai* in 1 Timothy is in the context of a warning against false teachers of the law. Paul reminded the young Christian leader in

[5] White, *Eros Defiled*, p. 128.

Ephesus that the law was good if a man used it properly. It was not made basically for good men but for lawbreakers, rebels, etc. Homosexual practice, like murder, adultery, slave trading, and lying, is contrary to sound doctrine. Perhaps that is precisely why people like Bailey and Blair are more dangerous to the whole matter of the gay problem in Western culture today than the drag queens who march through the streets of San Francisco. Their pretense of seriousness regarding the biblical text and their perversions of explicit biblical teaching on the subject cast them in the same mold as the false teachers against whom Paul wrote in his first letter to Timothy.

Surely in this passage Paul had the Decalogue in mind as he listed the sins that were contrary to sound doctrine. But the key idea in the Timothy passage is the role of the law in stimulating interest toward the gospel. The real ministry of the law is to show sinners their sin and the solution God has provided in the gospel. To say it again, the gospel is for the gay just as it is for the murderer, the lawbreaker, the liar, and the adulterer.

Evangelicals are often accused of using the Sodom account and the Levitical law on homosexuality to argue for contemporary legislation prohibiting homosexual practice in the nations of Western culture. Certainly, Christians who believe that such behavior is sinful ought to vote against laws permitting it just as they would vote against laws permitting or encouraging murder, adultery, slave trading, perjury, drunkenness, extortion, and the other sins in these two lists from the pen of the apostle Paul.

But it is not the legal aspect that is of importance, as Paul clearly pointed out in this passage. The New Testament concept is a recognition of the law as an instrument or tool to bring men to the gospel. The law was never intended for fanciful conjecture or interpretation on the part of the justified man, although it certainly does have a role in keeping human society in some semblance of order. Here again we run into the natural–special revelation connections of God as Creator and Redeemer thereby forcing us to consider our subject of homosexuality in both the natural and theological realms.

God's Offer of Hope

The evangelical message to the homosexual is a message of hope, not condemnation. Yes, homosexual behavior is a sin and God hates sin. But God also forgives sin and the most hopeful words in all of Scripture for a homosexual practitioner are found in 1 Corinthians 6:11: "And that is what some of you were. But you were washed, you were sanctified, you were justified in the name of the Lord Jesus Christ and by the Spirit of our God" (NIV). John Drakeford has described the change that Christ brought to the life of a former homosexual.

> The much propagated idea that the Christian religion condemns the homosexual and leaves him without hope is not borne out in Johnson's experience. In reality the uncompromising condemnation of Holy Writ helped Johnson "hit bottom" and then pushed him toward a new way of life. The same Bible that taught him the wrongness of homosexuality brought him his hope. His greatest encouragement and his basis for confidence in the future came from reading the Bible. Paul's letter to the Corinthians convinced him that he could be confident of a new way of life. After so many disappointing experiences, the

biblical statement that the Corinthians living as homosexuals in a depraved city had been changed and were not dedicated Christians became a ray penetrating the gathering gloom.[6]

To be sure the emotional problems that accompany homosexuality may not disappear immediately any more than other habits are always miraculously cured at the time of conversion. But it is of value for us to examine the three hopeful verbs of this beautiful eleventh verse—"washed, sanctified, justified."

All three words are in the aorist tense, emphasizing the definiteness of the work of the Lord in salvation. The first *(apelousasthe)* is in the middle voice and could very well be translated "you washed yourselves" or "you got yourselves washed," indicating a volitional act on the part of the sinner to accept God's offer to life-changing regeneration through the Spirit.

To be sanctified (in the New Testament sense) means to be set apart to the holy purposes of God; and to be justified means to be declared righteous before God's legal tribunal. All this is done in the name of the Lord Jesus Christ and by the Spirit of our God. It is free, it is available, it is guaranteed, and it is God's answer to the homosexual's problems. Robert Cowles had the idea clearly in mind when he said:

If the twisted emotions of the homosexual were not of his own making or incapable of change, then God could not justly condemn him. But if homosexuality is a sin—and the Bible is clear on this point—then God can change the homosexual because He came to save sinners.

[6]*Forbidden Love* (Waco, Tex.: Word Books, 1971), pp. 146–47.

> Christians condemn homosexuality because it is sin. But we hold out hope to the homosexual through the power of Christ Jesus.[7]

But even a definition of terms coupled with some basic understanding of the cause of homosexuality does not answer all of our questions. It is crucial also to grasp some of the distinctions that must be made as a result of a biblical understanding. Two of the most important differences—absolute versus relative morality, and propensity versus practice—are the subjects of our next chapter.

[7]"Gay as in Gomorrah," *The Christian Reader* (November-December 1947): 16.

CHAPTER 8

WHAT'S THE DIFFERENCE?

In June of 1977, Senator John Briggs of the California Legislature attempted to pass a resolution in support of Anita Bryant's position in the Dade County gay referendum fight. The resolution died in committee after homosexuals demonstrated outside the capitol building in Sacramento. The photo accompanying the news story showed a homosexual supporter holding a sign that read: "Jesus died for my sins not my sexuality."

That sign is indicative of the problems we face in grappling with the issues of homosexuality in our society. Differences are minimized; distinctions are blurred; definitions are confused. Of course, sexuality *per se* is not sin, but at what point does the perversion of natural sexuality become sin, and what is the difference between sin and sickness in dealing with various perversions?

In our confused society, we have become so fogged in the distinctions between good and bad, right and wrong, moral and immoral that many people no longer recognize that clearly definable distinctions exist. From business ethics to sexual morality we are a nation without norms, trapped in a miasma of relative confusion.

One of the questions that must be raised at the outset is whether homosexuality is by biblical implication a defiance of nature, Mosaic Law, or gospel. We have looked at passages that deal with the three eras when these were prominent, and one does not have to be a dispensationalist to recognize that divine government on earth before the time of Moses was largely a following of natural law, which then came to be supported by written law, and which ultimately was fulfilled in the gospel through the incarnate Son (Rom. 5:13-17).

Perhaps the central response to this pressing question is the unity of Scripture and the consistency of the God of Scripture. We should expect (and therefore should not be surprised to find) that the foundations of natural law are subsumed and specified in Mosaic commandments only to be ultimately fulfilled in the gospel—the gospel that provides the answer for helpless man who is unable to meet the demands of the two former authorities.

To put it another way, one cannot be right with God and at odds with God's creation; he cannot be living according to revealed truth and at the same time running counter to natural revelation—all truth is God's. One writer talks about the vertical and horizontal relationships being in line.

What is theologically noteworthy and kerygmatically "binding" in this exposition of Paul's (Romans 1:26f) is the statement that disorder in the vertical dimension (in the God-man relationship) is matched by a perversion on the horizontal level, not only within man himself (spirit-flesh relationship) but also in his interhuman contacts. One of the fundamental lines that runs through the Bible is that the analogy between the vertical and the horizontal relations is maintained and given theological foundation. An outstanding example of this two-dimensional view is the story of the tower of Babel (Genesis 11:1ff.) in which man's rebellion against the Creator (vertical movement) brings with it the "dispersion," that is, the destruction of human community and thus the perversion of the fellow-human relationship along with the confusion of tongues (horizontal movement).[1]

The same writer goes on to openly admit that "Paul is here rejecting homosexuality, otherwise he would not characterize it in this passage . . . as a symptom of original sin," but unfortunately he then falls into the trap of accommodation, blaming Paul's interpretation on Greek culture and concluding that since homosexuality cannot be cured it must be accepted. These latter contentions will be treated in another chapter, but of interest here is the author's willingness to admit that homosexuality is clearly a disruption of the natural order.

In this area of legitimate inquiry thus opened up the first thing that must be said is that for biblical thinking and the Christian thinking which follows biblical thought, it is impossible to think of homosexuality as having no ethical significance, as being a mere "vagary" or "sport" of nature. The fundamental order of creation makes it appear justifiable to speak of homosexuality as a "perversion"—in any case, if we begin with the understanding that this term implies no moral

[1]Cited in Burl A. DeLong, "A Critique of Current Evangelical Interpretation Regarding the Biblical Understanding of Homosexuality" (Master's Degree thesis, Dallas Theological Seminary, 1977), pp. 279–80.

depreciation whatsoever and that it is used purely theologically in the sense that homosexuality is in every case *not* in accord with the order of creation.[2]

The semantic juggling in the above paragraph of the words "moral" and "theological" is quite stunning. Surely no Christian would admit that any God-ordained morality could be operative in the world apart from God's revelation, and that links morality (or certainly Christian morality) inseparably with theology. Several important distinctions need to be made in order to sort out these theological implications.

The Difference Between Absolute and Relative Morality

The Christian believes in absolute standards of truth, ethics, and morality. To be sure, his interpretation of that absolute biblical standard at any time and place may be based on faulty exegesis and interpretation. Nevertheless, there are some things on which conservative Christianity has always stood firm. The world on the other hand operates its entire system on the basis of relative truth, relative ethics, and relative morality. In waning shades of Joseph Fletcher's *Situation Ethics: The New Morality,* Ralph Blair has written his commendation of homosexuality in a simple sentence that appeals to the principle of relativism: "From a biblical viewpoint, there is only one prescription for conduct and attitude, and that is this real concern and demonstration for the real welfare of ourselves and of other persons regardless of

[2]Ibid., p. 282.

our anatomies and regardless of our physical activity."[3]

But love is *not* enough—truth is also important. To be sure, homosexuality is not necessarily a worse sin than the others that appear in the same lists in these three New Testament passages.

And some will say, "But aren't some homosexuals nice, good, loving people?" No doubt they are, but as Harold Lindsell puts it:

> Good feelings cannot deliver him from the judgment of God. If he does not repent, he is doomed, but he is not alone. So are all other unrepentant sinners. God is no respecter of persons: he is also no respecter of one's sexual appetites. Hell will be partially populated by "caring, honest, whole persons" who are proud that they are gay.[4]

This whole question of homosexual behavior being ethically correct because it operates from love comfortably makes the leap from a general position of relative morality to the more specific and active commitment of what we have come to call "situation ethics." Christians wonder how (in the light of scriptural teaching) the idea that homosexual behavior is not wrong can be seriously entertained. The answer is that those who accept such a position assume that biblical teaching can be interpreted using the assumptions of situational ethics. Any discussion of text and exegesis are treated with a condescending attitude that makes those of a different viewpoint feel that such matters are only straw men that need to be destroyed so the "real" issue of love can be under-

[3]Blair, "Evangelical Look at Homosexuality": 9.

[4]"Homosexuals and the Church," *Christianity Today* (28 September 1973): 12.

stood. Note the clever manipulation of Christ's teaching in the following excerpt:

> We need the Bible as a source to understand Christ—but we need to spend more time observing His Spirit as related there rather than the "letter of the law" given by His followers in attempting to spread His message.

> Pick up an edition of the Bible with Christ's recorded statements. printed in red. Study only His words, comparing His positive approach with the often negative approach found elsewhere throughout the Scriptures. Notice His emphasis on love—His silence on the means of sex, but concern only with the motives behind it.[5]

It would be good if we had time and space here to discuss all the assumptions of situational ethics, but we do not. John Montgomery writes of six basic propositions of situational ethics. The ones most affecting the homosexual issue are that love constitutes the "only intrinsic good" and it is the "ultimate norm of Christian decision-making."[6] These assumptions imply that no act in and of itself is intrinsically evil. The rightness or the wrongness of anything is extrinsic, relative, and dependent upon the circumstances. The overriding concern is to do what would be the most "loving thing" for everyone concerned.

With its "love as panacea" the new morality has strong emotional appeal. But to claim love as the solution to anything and everything is not only un-

[5]Kim Stablinski, "Homosexuality, What the Bible Does and Does Not Say," *The Ladder* (July 1969).

[6]*Situation Ethics: A Dialogue between Joseph Fletcher and John Montgomery* (Minneapolis: Dimension Books, 1972), p. 25

sympathetic, it is un-Christian. Christian theism does not deny the supremacy of love or profess that God loves homosexuals less than He does heterosexuals. The problem is what proponents of situational ethics, particularly those who believe in "Christian" situational ethics, mean by the term "love." Their understanding of love and morality is not derived either from the Bible in general or from the ministry of Jesus in particular.

Religious proponents of the new morality go to great lengths to try to establish that Christ was against "law morality"—that Christ did not hold to any intrinsic morality. This is impossible to sustain while staying true to the New Testament account of Christ. For example, consider one of the key passages from the Sermon on the Mount: "Whosoever therefore shall break one of these least commandments, and shall teach men so, he shall be called the least in the kingdom of heaven: but whosoever shall do and teach them, the same shall be called great in the kingdom of heaven" (Matt. 5:19). In the same context, Jesus stated that He did not "come to abolish them [the law] but to fulfill them" (Matt. 5:17, NIV).

Those who use Christ as an example of One who preached situational ethics portray Him as a rebel against the legalism of His people—One who was trying to do away with the Law. However, the key to the issue is determining exactly what Jesus was *for* and what He was *against*. He was not against the Torah. When He opposed the legalism of the Pharisees, it was opposition to traditional Mishnaic legalism. All of Christ's so-called oppositions to the Torah are oppositions to legalistic accretions or attitudes that developed after the setting forth of the Torah itself.

For Christ there was no conflict between law and love. The gospels are full of accounts in which Christ gave illustrations from the Law about what people ought to do. He even spoke of love in terms of fulfilling the Law. In other words, the Bible sets forth moral absolutes that inform and guide love in its exercise.

So situational ethics discounts the issue of depravity and man's inability to know what pleases God apart from revelation. By its own admission, it is weak in the areas of guilt, sin, repentance, and forgiveness. Human growth and responsibility require the internalization of external authority. The biblical perspective on morality does not set law and gospel against each other in such a way that the gospel is preferable to the law. The simple fact is that without law one demonstrates not love but anarchy.[7]

Nowhere is this more evident than when it comes to answering the question, "Just what constitutes my neighbor's good?" If approached situationally, anything could be interpreted to be for a neighbor's good. As Fletcher asserts, "Lying could be more Christian than telling the truth since the only virtue in telling the truth is telling love."[8] With this open-ended use of "love," any of the vices in 1 Corinthians 6:9 or 1 Timothy 1:9,10 could be justified. Not just homosexuality, but fornication, adultery, theft, and greed could all be justified as means to a worthy end.

Where does one stop if biblical absolutes are reduced to relative alternatives in the name of "love"? Clearly, love requires principles to guide its impulses. The claim of historic Christianity is that bibli-

[7]Tom F. Driver, "Love Needs Law," *Religion and Life* (Spring 1966): 200.

[8]*Situation Ethics*, p. 38.

cal revelation constitutes a transcendent word from God-established ethical norms. It is a revelatory ethic rather than a situational ethic.

No one would argue that "love is that which seeks good for the object loved." But what is "good" in the opinion of one is not "good" in the opinion of another. The nature of "good" is the dilemma of situational ethics. There is no objective way to answer this question without propositional revealed truth. For the Christian committed to the Bible, good is the will of God; good is what God wants for me. Love then is whatever seeks the will of God for the person or object loved.

If the passages surveyed in earlier chapters genuinely teach that homosexual behavior is not the will of God (and I believe they do), then to initiate a homosexual relationship with one's neighbor is not seeking the will of God in his life, and therefore it can never be the loving thing to do.

The Difference Between Discrimination and Oppression

Do evangelicals discriminate against homosexuals? Yes, they do, but discrimination is not oppression. The Christian is forced to discriminate, not on the basis of natural sex, color, or ethnic origin, for these are things that God has designed. We discriminate on the basis of sin and righteousness, and sin is precisely the issue of homosexuality. The church does discriminate against atheists, agnostics, fornicators, adulterers, drunkards, and there is no question that such are not welcome into the family of God except through repentance and conversion. But this discrimination is hardly oppressive and that distinction must be clearly maintained.

Furthermore, the *discrimination* of which we

speak here is not to be confused with the more common ethnic connotation of that term. Of course, gays would like very much to line up with blacks, chicanos, and women and present themselves as just one more oppressed minority group. Interviewed in *The Wittenburg Door,* Anita Bryant referred to a statement by Ted Ford Johnson, a black leader in Dade County.

> He says that when you are black, it sticks. Homosexuality is a matter of conduct. To compare it to the hard-fought bloody battle of civil rights is a disgrace, he said. Homosexuality has nothing to do with civil rights. They aren't born that way. And I think that once the people in Dade County were educated, the black community, the Jews, and everyone else voted accordingly. They saw it not as a civil rights issue. It was a moral one. Homosexuals come in on the banner of civil rights, but it is just a bold-faced lie. And I have found that most blacks resent it.[9]

An editorial in the same issue of the *Wittenburg Door* emphasized that the discrimination is definitely linked to a theological premise that cannot be divorced from historic natural law and levitical code.

> Two observations or qualifications need to be made. One is that the Holiness Code must never be torn from its theological context to be seen only in a cultural setting and thus relegated to another time and place. Its theological setting is the Genesis accounts of Creation and Fall and the Abrahamic Covenant previously mentioned. The intent of the law was to set the people apart from

[9]"Door Interview: Anita Bryant," *Wittenburg Door,* no. 39 (October-November 1977): 13.

the nations, Egypt and Canaan; to distinguish Israel as a people Holy unto God. We should not be too quick to think that we understand fully the reasons for those laws in their original setting, and can therefore deny their relevance to us. In this connection, it may be of significance to note the qualitatively different punishment given for the sin of intercourse during menstruation, which is exile (Leviticus 20:18), as opposed to the punishment of sins such as incest, adultery, homosexuality, and bestiality, which is death (Leviticus 20:10-14).[10]

The Difference Between Propensity and Practice

It is quite customary today to talk about homosexuals as either inverts or perverts. *Invert* is the term used to describe a "constitutional" or endogenous homosexual whereas *pervert* refers to a heterosexual person who engages in homosexual activity. Such a distinction immediately raises the question of cause, which we must postpone until the first part of the next chapter, but suffice it here to say that we grant the existence of the invert but are extremely reluctant to attribute his inversion to organic or genetic factors.

The argument regarding propensity or practice would seem on the surface to be a biological, psychological, or sociological issue. But it is also a theological question, because if homosexuals can argue that their condition is hereditary or constitutional, they can throw the entire question out of the arena of biblical restraints. The Bible does not talk about tendency, preference, or life-style, but about homosexual acts. Klaus Bockmühl talks about the difference

[10]"Editorial," *Wittenburg Door* (October-November 1977): 22.

between propensity and practice as being the difference between sickness and sin:

> In cases where a fixation has already occurred through early childhood experience or other factors, we can only agree with the Anglican report: such a fixation relieves the homosexual of accountability of his homosexual *propensity,* but it cannot relieve him of the responsibility for his homosexual acts. We must always make this distinction.[11]

But let's back up for a moment. When the American Psychiatric Association eliminated homosexuality as a mental disorder, it substituted a new category titled "Sexual Orientation Disturbance."[12] This new category was for "individuals whose sexual interests are directed primarily toward people of the same sex and who are either disturbed by, in conflict with, or wish to change their sexual orientation."[13] In other words, homosexuality becomes a problem only when the person cannot accept it for what it is.

Almost all definitions, whether they view homosexuality as sin or sickness, center on the pervert rather than the invert. It would appear that thinking Christians dealing with the subject of homosexuality today have great sympathy for inverts and are willing to examine with them all the possible avenues to discovery of cause and cure. But that is hardly what the gay liberation movement is after. Blair wants a

---

[11]"Homosexuality and Biblical Perspective," *Christianity Today* (16 February 1973): 14.

[12]*Diagnostic and Statistical Manual of Mental Health,* 2nd ed. (Washington D.C.: American Psychiatric Association, 1975), p. vi.

[13]Ibid., p. 44.

full justification of homosexual *practice* and cares
not for what the church may or may not say regarding
propensity.

> Some evangelical leaders may show some con-
> cern that homosexuals no longer be discrimi-
> nated against in terms of their vocational careers,
> the criminal law, and harassment. Usually, how-
> ever, these same leaders insist that homosexual
> men and women must not act upon their sexual
> desires. But it must be observed that the Bible is
> severe in its denunciation of the asceticism which
> demands and seeks to promote and enforce ab-
> stinence from a thing which should be received
> with thanksgiving, as one's sexuality should
> be.[14]

He obviously begs the question, assuming the natu-
ralness of homosexuality and then applying biblical
injunctions against homosexual asceticism as he de-
fines it.

Make no mistake about it, the so-called "gay
evangelicals" argue vehemently that homosexual
Christians have too long been living under a burden
of prejudice from the "straight" church. Because of
this injustice the love of God has been nullified for all
sincere homosexual believers. Consequently, they
believe that homosexual Christians must learn to
stand firm in the love of God and that peace and life
will then be realized as they accept their "God ordained" homosexual life-style. "Imagine: Your
homosexual self is a part of you—the you God loves.
You are free to be His most faithful son or daughter

[14]Blair, "Evangelical Look at Homosexuality": 2.

within your very own sexual identity. He does not ask us to give up our sexual identities."[15]

There is an obvious and continuing relationship in Scripture between homosexuality and adultery, both perversions of God-ordained sexuality. To be sure, the church needs to welcome repentant homosexuals just as it would welcome repentant adulterers. By the same token, however, the homosexual who has an ounce of commitment to the authority of Scripture is not more free to engage in homosexual relations than the many heterosexuals who are not married or who for some other reason are unable to engage in sexual relations with a marriage partner are free to engage in extramarital relations. Surely even Blair would not argue that Christian heterosexuals should feel free to fornicate when and where they wish if there is a "love" relationship and their propensity leads them in that direction to satisfy a God-ordained sexuality!

So the invert still has a choice to make whatever the cause of his inversion. Those who reject the biological argument are relieved of the requirement to think of propensity as automatic commitment. I like the way Ben Patterson and Curt Anderson spell it out.

> Human nature, ontologically speaking, is not some fixed essence or quantity. From the biblical point of view our identity is always seen as being relational. It is only in relation to God that we know who we are. To regard as "nature" what a sick society and pathological family unity may have produced is to elevate the creation (and a fallen one at that) to the level of the Creator. I believe the Apostle Paul had some choice words for that.

[15]Ibid., p. 10.

Homosexual inversion is not a sin. The decision to act it out is. The homosexual invert is a sinner for the same reasons, not more and not less, than the rest of us. We are all caught up in the same net of rebellion, and we all have chosen our own special repertoire out of the seemingly endless variety of ways to avoid the Holy Will of God.[16]

Blair and others would have us believe that a legalistic pressing of biblical injunctions against homosexuality prohibits gays from lives of happiness and joy. If the church would just get off their backs, we are told, they could learn to enjoy their God-given sexuality and lead "normal" lives. But the record of those who have experienced the inner conflict hardly supports that contention. Indeed, if we are correct about the theological implications of the biblical text, it would be impossible for a "Christian homosexual" to be genuinely happy while practicing homosexual acts.

One admitted homosexual pastor wrote *Christianity Today* regarding the dilemma of his status. I thought the following was the most meaningful paragraph of the letter:

Homosexuality is a manifestation of the lust of the flesh, never, in my opinion, of the love set forth in the Word of God. Love binds two people together and is a manifestation of the love of God. The love of a man and a woman draws them together to become husband and wife, to be joined as one in sexual union. To try to fit people of the same sex into the biblical picture of marriage is impossible at every point. The sex act in marriage is the ultimate expression of love. The sex act performed apart from marriage falls short

[16]*Wittenburg Door* (October–November 1977): 24.

of this ultimate expression and leaves much to be desired. Often, if not always, it leaves both persons with a sense of guilt and lack of fulfillment. This is true of loveless marriages, of masturbation, and of homosexual activity.[17]

[17]"Letter from a Homosexual," *Christianity Today* (1 March 1968): 23.

CHAPTER 9

HOW DID I GET THIS WAY?

The social impact of homosexuality in Western culture is tremendous. Though the Christian must approach the subject from a theological point of reference, he cannot ignore the social implications anymore than this book could be complete without raising some of those issues on the practical level. Surely any practical discussion of the issue must first attempt to deal with the cause(s) of homosexuality.

Three Proposals

If we accept the presupposition that homosexual *practice* is sin, we still are faced with a question of what causes homosexual *propensity*. One of the factors identified by psychologists is sometimes called "traumatic homosexuality." There certainly is sufficient evidence that *psychic predisposition* to homosexuality does exist. A physically or psychologically absent father, a dominating mother, or some other kind of psychological trauma at an early age can conceivably cause homosexuality in an individual who would otherwise have been heterosexual. Klaus Bockmühl quotes Dr. Richard Houser in an extraordinary study made for the British Home Ministry entitled *The Homosexual Society* (1962).

> . . . a narrow line divides abnormal from normal behavior, and there is great danger of crossing this line during adolescence, when a person passes through a phase of sexual ambivalence. This is the time when a homosexual fixation of emotional and social development can most easily take place. We must firmly repudiate the myth that such a fixation is necessarily irreversible. Houser produces evidence to show that only 4 to 8 per cent of the active homosexuals are exclusively homosexual in their orientation; the far greater number are bisexual. This brings the real problem into focus: it lies not in the existence of a minuscule number of people who really might have a strong predisposition to homosexuality but in the greater number of those who have *chosen* homosexual behavior, so that homosexuality threatens to become an aggressive social epidemic.[1]

Another causative factor of homosexuality is *non traumatic learned behavior*. (Obviously, one could argue that traumatic experiences also produce learned behavior, so we must introduce the adjective "non-traumatic.") Psychiatrist Charles Young has emphasized the learned behavior approach.

> I am persuaded that homosexuality is mainly a learned condition, and that anything learned may be altered by further learning. I do not believe that anyone is damned from the time of his conception to become homosexual. I agree with Freud in his "free contributions to the theory of

[1]Bockmühl, "Homosexuality and Biblical Perspective": 17.

sex" that every person has the potential to become homosexual. If a person encourages and cultures the deviant urges, which can be aroused in all of us, he is on the way to a life of sexual perversion.[2]

Still a third cause of homosexuality is the *deliberate selection* of a gay life-style. To be sure, the propensity had to be there, but the cultivation and development of homosexuality in oneself or others is precisely the area of sin I have attempted to explicate in detail above. It is at this point that we leave the problem of sickness and enter the area of sin. Martin Hoffman, staff psychiatrist at the Center for Special Problems in San Francisco, urged America's teachers (in what is probably the most widely read journal for public educators) to stop trying to *cure* homosexuals and begin *accepting* them. He objected to the claim that homosexuals can be made heterosexual and said, "my conviction is that we are going to have to accept homosexuality as a valid way of life and remove the social and legal stigmas that are now attached to it."[3]

And therein lies the problem. With psychologists and religionists telling homosexuals that they need not, should not, and probably cannot change, it is no wonder that they select a militant gay deviation and announce themselves as the most oppressed minority group in Western culture. *Homosexual propensity may indeed be a sickness, but homosexual practice and promotion is not physical illness, mental derangement, or an acceptable variant life-style—it is sin.* And it is precisely on this ground that

[2] "Homosexuality and the Campus, *HIS* (February 1966): 24.
[3] "Homosexuality," *Today's Education NEA Journal* (November 1970): 46.

the church must wage its battle. But what about biological causes? Aren't homosexuals just born that way? And if so, how can they help being what God has made them?

Homosexuals Are Made Not Born

˃ I have already stated several times that biological derivation or genetic determinism is not an acceptable answer to the question of cause of homosexuality. This was a very popular view in earlier days and was held by many researchers, some of whom were listed by Albert Ellis:

> Writers such as Carpenter (1911, 1914), Bloch (1908), H. Ellis (1936), Forel (1907), Hirschfeld (1920), Kraft-Ebing (1886), and Robinson (1914) stoutly held that either some or all homosexuals are born rather than conditioned to be attracted to members of their own sex and that hormonal or genic imbalances lie at the bottom of confirmed homosexualism. Many later writers also echo these views on the primacy of constitutional factors in homosexuality. . . .[4]

Of course, militant gays, especially those who want to show some semblance of commitment to biblical evangelicalism, are soundly supportive of the biological cause viewpoint. If indeed God permits homosexuals to be born that way, then homosexuality may very well be a natural form of behavior and inversion an acceptable life-style.

Howard A. Eyrich sums up the research negating the genetic determinism theory including rejection of

[4]*Homosexuality: Its Causes and Cure* (New York: Lyle Stewart Inc., 1965), p. 21.

the brain damage hypothesis, the historical and cultural hypothesis, and the hormonal imbalance hypothesis. He argues that the generalization that homosexuality has been found throughout history in about the same ratio of the population and therefore must be biologically inborn is based upon extremely dubious foundations.

> A far safer generalization would be that, since human beings are born anatomically male or female, and since the vast majority appear heterosexually, human beings are born to be heterosexual. From the available historical and cultural evidence, a third generalization is also possible: All humans are born ambisexually, with a majority choosing hetereosexuality and the minority homosexuality. If the evidence allows these alternate conclusions, can there be any doubt of its uselessness in establishing genetic determination of homosexuality?[5]

In a sense the hormone theory, which treats endocrine immaturity in males, is different from the genetic theory in that it is based on the assumption that the sex drive is under the control of hormones and that the choice of sexual object is also controlled by hormones. The chief hormone for man is testosterone and for women it is estradiol. It is believed that when the ratio of testosterone production to estradiol in the male is below a certain ratio, this will predispose him to be a homosexual. Usually the amount of hormones measured from urinary hormone levels are assumed to be a good indicator of the hormone level in the blood plasma. It is the plasma

[5]"Hope for the Homosexual" *The Journal of Pastoral Practice* (November 1977): 23.

level that affects the sexual behavior. Generally speaking, homosexuals do register lower levels of testosterone than heterosexuals.

But the researchers themselves question the meaning of the evidence and cannot determine if the lower testosterone level is the cause of homosexuality or if the homosexuality is the cause of the lower testosterone level. After detailed research on the subject, Raymond L. Tibe concludes:

> From this information, it can be safely stated that the data do not indicate that homosexuality is the result of an endocrine imbalance. This is not to say that there is no evidence for the existence of a physiological difference between homosexual and heterosexual males. Yet, the meaning of this difference, if it truly exists, is still in doubt.[6]

A second major constitutional theory is the genetic, and it divides into two sub-categories, the inheritance view, and the intersex view that argues that a genetic interchange (in which a male possesses a genetic endowment of a female yet is morphologically male) is the cause of homosexuality.

We have neither space nor purpose here to make a detailed study of monozygotic and dizygotic. The major problem with these studies has been their inconsistent results. Environmental factors continue to be major variables in the research and the inheritance theory does not gain anything like general validity from the studies.

Evidence for the intersex theory comes from the "sib-ratio" research and studies of direct chro-

[6]"A Critical Evaluation of the Rationale Used in Support of Male Homosexuality Among Christians (Master's Degree Thesis, Trinity Evangelical Divinity School, 1973), p. 23.

mosomal sexing and checking. Sib-ratio research is based on the hypothesis that if homosexuals are genetic females in male bodies, then there should be a higher ratio of males among the siblings of families that have homosexual children. Studies were conducted by surveying hundreds of normal families and determining the total boy-girl sibling ratio within them.

Once this control group had been established hundreds of families with homosexual children were surveyed to determine their boy-girl ratios. Results were then compared to see if there was any significant difference in the sib-ratios between the homosexual and control families. Again, the studies have been inconclusive and Tibe remarks:

> In light of these criticisms, it is fair to question the meaning of the sib-ratio research produced to date and to state that no adequate evidence for validity of the intersex theory has been produced from this type of research so far. From the previously mentioned material chromosome checking, it is also apparent that there is no direct evidence from these studies for the intersex theory. Therefore, the theory of intersex must be rejected at this point for lack of evidence.[7]

So the only conclusion fitting the evidence is that homosexuality is a learned behavior. That still leaves it open to a number of causes as I indicated earlier in the chapter, but it carries now a responsibility for any actions that follow the propensity. John White emphasizes the problems developed by patterns of behavior—the simple matter of habituation.

Let a young person once experience pleasure

[7]Ibid.

from sex play with someone of his or her own sex, and the sex play will become that much more appealing the next time. The vulnerability of the mother-dominated young man I described above lies precisely here. Because his sexual urges are (at least temporarily) blocked in one direction, they will more easily find an outlet in the other. And because it is easier for him to form deep intimate relationships with someone of his own sex, his sexual urges may be awakened in that context. The pleasure and relief he experiences from a sexual relationship with another man will "stamp in" this pattern of behavior, making it more natural for him in the future.[8]

White's point is that it really makes little difference how the propensity toward homosexuality is started as long as we recognize that it cannot be attributed to genetic or inherited physiology. Environmental conditioning is a major factor in developing homosexuality regardless of what forms the conditioning may take.

Perhaps the work of Karlen provides the strongest evidence for the argument that homosexuality is a learned behavior.[9] Behavior that is learned by neurotic adjustment or whatever other means can be unlearned. A person may be a confirmed liar, but he has chosen to lie at some point along the line and therefore can choose not to lie through the appropriate treatment or help. Likewise, a homosexual can choose homosexuality or choose to leave it.

Are There Different Kinds of Homosexuality?

Perhaps further discussion needs to be offered re-

---

[8]*Eros Defiled* (Downers Grove, Ill.: InterVarsity Press, 1977), p. 117.

[9]Cited in DeLong, "Critique of Homosexuality."

garding this matter of *types* of homosexuals. I have attempted to argue throughout the book that we are dealing only with people who commit homosexual acts, and I have attempted to make a significant distinction between "propensity" and "practice." There might also be a distinction here between sickness and sin, though the experts are hardly agreed on how to handle the matter of classification. It is important, however, to make a distinction between terms like *bisexual,* a condition in which male or female seems to find satisfaction and some degree of fulfillment in sexual activities with members of either sex; *transvestite,* a term applying to a person who makes every effort to masquerade as a member of the opposite sex; and *transsexual,* a person (like Dr. Renee Richards) who actually endures surgery and change of appropriate hormones to alter his or her sex.

Categorization is not only difficult but probably impossible when one is dealing with the total issue of homosexuality. One writer preferred a ranking by degrees.

Lionell Ovesey, the psychoanalyst who invented the term *pseudo-homosexual* (one who fears he is a homosexual but isn't), describes different grades or degrees of homosexuality in men. The range is from men who are exclusively heterosexual through those who have only occasionally had relations with men and whose "preferred mode of behavior is heterosexual" (that is, with women) to those who have never had anything but homosexual relations and are therefore "exclusively homosexual." Somewhere in the middle are men I have already referred to as bisexual. They are often married and with children, leading a gay life on the side. Because secrecy

has to cloak their homosexual activities, they are
known in the gay world as "closet queens."[10]

Any categorization of homosexuals by their attitudes or appearance is a plastic superimposition
upon reality. But there may be some value in getting
away from an overall universal classification that
distorts the real differences that do exist among
homosexuals. *Time* magazine once attempted a classification that still might be of some help, although a
great deal has transpired in social attitudes toward
homosexuality since the article was written, and it is
merely a "pop" language approach.

Time talked about *the blatant homosexual* and
called him the "eunuch like caricature of femininity"
who may either be "the catty hair dresser or the
lisping, limp-wristed interior decorator" and the
"sado-masochistic leather jacket and chain types"
who hide their deviation by what they consider to be
overt masculinity. Such stereotyped "queers" are
really a small minority of the homosexual community
however, and *Time* gave more attention to *the
secret-lifer*. In this broad segment of the homosexual
community could be many young and middle-aged
men or women who in "real life" wear wedding rings
and dress conservatively but under the camouflage
are homosexual in preference and, whenever possible, in practice.

Time also spoke about *the desperate* who haunt
public toilets and are "unable to face the slightest
strains of sustaining a serious human relationship";
the adjusted who rarely represent the gay crowd that
we see today; *the bisexual* who fakes heterosexual

[10]"The Homosexual: Newly Visible, Newly Understood,"
Time, 31 October 1969, pp. 61–64.

relations and really prefers homosexual contacts; and *the situational-experimental* type who engages in homosexual acts without any really deep motivation.[11]

The blatant homosexual of our day, however, is not the "limp-wristed interior decorator," but rather the gay activist who has taken his cause into public and into politics. So in 1971, *Newsweek* could run a special article entitled "The Militant Homosexual," which identified how the gay liberation movement was bringing homosexuals out of the closets and restrooms and into the streets. That action, of course, raises public protest just as it does public promotion, and *Newsweek* could ask a very legitimate question:

> What all this suggests is a central problem that gay liberation usually chooses to ignore: If the movement succeeds in creating an image of "normality" for homosexuals in the society at large, would it encourage more homosexually-inclined people—particularly young people—to follow their urges without hesitation?[12]

The answer can only be yes if false theories regarding cause and cure are allowed to influence the thinking of homosexuals who want to change. The key has already been stated—learned behavior *can* be unlearned.

[11]Ibid.
[12]"The Militant Homosexual," *Newsweek,* 23 August 1971, p. 48.

CHAPTER 10

FEELINGS, NOTHING MORE THAN FEELINGS

Does the word "gay" really apply to homosexuals? Militant gay activists would have us believe that the only way a homosexual can find happiness in life is to be fully accepted by the rest of society and be allowed to practice and promote his cause as he wishes. The American Institute of Family Relations is not at all hesitant to speak to this question. Psychologists and psychiatrists there view homosexuality as

> . . . an illness of social proportions, national significance, and serious portent. . . . As a preliminary to any successful campaign for mental health, energetic measures should be taken to shut off the present homosexual propaganda in which many well-meaning clergymen have been led to participate. The newspapers and other mass media might take the responsibility for refusing to let the homosexuals publicly call themselves "gay." . . . In short, homosexuality is, for every possible reason, neither necessary nor desirable. It is a definite evil, from every point of view, and should be looked on as such. It is not to be supposed that it can be eliminated easily and

at once and forever, but an educated public opinion should face up to it honestly and vigorously.[1]

John Drakeford recommends integrity therapy to
help the homosexual but reprimands the church for
not holding the solid ground of its historic stance on
the issue: "Nothing could be plainer," he insists,
"than the attitude laid down in the Bible, which the
Christians are deliberately violating—the first in-
junction being that homosexuality cannot be toler-
ated, the second that it can be changed ('cured') and
that the Christian obligation is to see to it that it be
cured, as Saint Paul more than once demanded of
them."[2]

Part of the whole problem of inner feelings and
attitudes is the matter of sexual identity. I referred
above to transsexuals, and it is obvious that sex-
change surgery is being performed at an increasing
rate.

Dr. Paul Weinberg, professor of psychiatry,
obstetrics, and gynecology at the University of
Texas Medical School in San Antonio, says that
"many who want the operation are merely rejecting
their homosexuality. They are people who are socially uncomfortable as homosexuals and prefer
identities as transsexuals."[3] Weinberg estimates that
ten thousand sex change operations have been performed since the early sixties and emphasizes the
significance of parental attitudes in developing a
child's sexual identity. What a child is named, how

[1]Paul Popenoe, "Are Homosexuals Necessary?" American
Institute of Family Relations, publication 542, pp. 3–4.
[2]*Forbidden Love* (Waco, Tex.: Word Books, 1971).
[3]*The Miami Herald*, 12 December 1977, p. 8A.

he is dressed, how he is treated by his parents, how the parents relate to each other as well as to him—all of these and a hundred other behaviors enforce feelings of gender.

Weinberg makes it very clear that a loving, caring home environment will rarely produce problems of sexual identity and emphasizes again what I have suggested several times, namely that while the roots of homosexual behavior are too varied to pinpoint, they are clearly not biological. According to Weinberg, "The hormonal set-up in homosexuals is exactly the same as in heterosexuals."[4]

It is certainly no effort to impugn motives that leads many experts on the subject to repeatedly emphasize that the word "gay" is an unfortunate designation for people who are suffering from deep emotional problems. (There are of course records of long-standing homosexual relationships that have brought obvious positive results to the partners. One would be foolish to generalize that *all* "gays" are not gay.) How then did the term get adopted so widely? William D. Rodgers offers three possibilities.

> One version has it that "gay" was applied to homosexuals in the theatre as early as the 1700s. There is no record of the reason of the application. It has been suggested it was due to the "sportive" nature of the homophiles it described.
>
> The *Dictionary of American Slang,* compiled by Wentworth and Flexner, seems to infer that it is in some way associated with "gay-cat," sometimes used in speaking of a homosexual jazz musician.

[4]Ibid.

Still a third version gives credit to the American ex-Patriot, Gertrude Stein, who was a celebrated lesbian, for importing it to English usage from French.

Whatever is the case, homosexuals themselves have adopted it with fervor. They say it gives a homosexual a positive feeling about himself. The press has been quick to aid and abet their linguistic cause. So now we have "gay rights," "gay pride," "gay parades," and "gay bars."

The truth is that homosexuals as a social class are no more "merry," "glad," or "joyful" than the rest of us. On the strength of the evidence, they are a lot less so.[5]

Recruitment

Both during and since the Dade County battle, the organization known as Save Our Children (SOC) has been accused of improperly propagating the motto, "Since homosexuals cannot reproduce, they must recruit to freshen their ranks." SOC states that the Los Angeles Police Department recently reported that twenty-five thousand male youth, age seventeen or younger, in that city alone have been recruited into a homosexual ring to provide sex for adult male customers. One boy, just twelve years old, was described as a one-thousand-dollar-a-day prostitute. Gays respond that they seek out *each other,* not straights to turn into homosexuals.[6]

New York sociologist Edward Sagarin reminds us that public attention to gays and their message that "groovy guys make groovy stars" leads impression-

[5]*The Gay Invasion* (Denver: Accent Books, 1977), p. 49.
[6]*The Miami Herald,* 20 March 1977, p. 9D.

able adolescents to think it might just be great to be gay. Sagarin insists that if we showed all the problems connected with homosexuality rather than extolling its virtues, "more adolescents with homosexual tendencies might seek to change instead of resolving their confusion by accepting the immediate warm security that tells them they are normal."[7]

Paul Popenoe supports the SOC conclusion when he says that the gay community "can only be kept alive by a continual recruiting of new victims."[8]

Sociologist Judson T. Landis once questioned eighteen hundred college students of whom one third reported an experience with at least one sexual deviate; and in the case of men, eighty-four percent of these episodes represented a homosexual approach—in two thirds of the instances when the boys were younger than sixteen years of age. Landis also indicated that the epidemic increase of venereal disease was due in an astonishingly large percentage of cases to homosexual contacts.[9]

This is an issue that comes under repeated attack by gays who imply that they certainly are not actively recruiting and just want to be left alone. But anyone who has observed the behavior of militant gays on television or read reports of their activities could hardly swallow that line. Obviously, closet gays or bisexuals have little motivation toward recruitment and are probably not a menace to society in general. But the attractiveness of the youthful form seems to have more impact for the homosexual than the het-

[7]"The Militant Homosexual," *Newsweek,* p. 48.
[8]Popenoe, "Are Homosexuals Necessary?" p. 2.
[9]"Experiences of 500 Children with Adult Sexual Deviation," *Psychiatric Quarterly Supplement* (Utica, N.Y.: State Hospital's Press, 1956).

erosexual. This surely must be true when one talks about arousal of sexual appetites for relations with a child of the same sex.

This is not to imply that all homosexuals are child molesters nor to suggest that heterosexual offenders are less of a danger to society. But even if there were one hundred heterosexual child molesters for every one homosexual child molester, it would not be reasonable to argue in favor of advancing the cause of that one.

Rodgers argues there is a discernible pattern that runs through the case histories of homosexuals, and he says "homosexuals have developed their own U.S.P. [unique selling proposition]." It is a pitch that takes advantage of the basic need to feel uniquely individual and couples it with the inferiority complexes we all have in order to create "The Difference Package."

> The Difference Package as an appeal to young people is dynamite. Adolescence is a terribly confused period in most people's lives. There are drastic hormonal and physical changes taking place, producing strange new emotions and sensations which heighten the teenager's feeling of being set apart from all others. The process would be hard for the mature mind to understand and cope with; for the immature adolescent it is almost impossible. And when an authoritarian figure comes along—another student, a social worker, a physician, a teacher—and ties all the frustration in one neat ball and labels it all "homosexuality," the prognosis makes sense, especially to the overly confused child whose body is on the verge of adulthood.[10]

[10]Rodgers, *The Gay Invasion,* p. 120.

The feelings of abnormality, the rejection by society, the dissatisfaction with one's self, all combine to drive the homosexual's urge for conquest or control of another's body to a greater height even than that experienced by heterosexuals.

Many straights have problems understanding the loathsome longings of the homosexual. They are repulsed by the very thought of sexual techniques commonly used by gays. We must remember that starving people in abnormal situations have eaten rats—and in extreme cases—even other human beings. The power of their hunger changed their attitudes entirely and the whole issue of ethics became completely confused. A normal, comfortably fed person reading about cannibalism practiced by a starving survivor of a shipwreck or airplane crash is nauseated because he cannot practice empathy with that starving man any more than a straight can think with the mind of a gay. What sickens a normal person may appear very attractive to a homosexual.

Ostracism

Without doubt ostracism is less of a problem for homosexuals now than ever before. They are receiving greater "understanding" and certainly wider toleration than at any time in the history of this country. Whether or not that is good is the whole thrust of this book; nevertheless, it is a fact. One news magazine predicts that "the prospect is that the activists will continue gradually to win more and more of the civil rights that have been denied to homosexuals in the past, and with these gains perhaps an increasing degree of public tolerance."[11]

[11]"Gays and the Law," *Newsweek,* 25 October 1976, p. 103.

Gays no longer want to be viewed as "queer" but accepted as a part of normal society. Obviously, they are making great strides toward that goal, and this raises a very difficult issue for the Christian. On the one hand, he understands well enough the biblical command to accept other people for what they are and to love them in and through Christ Jesus. On the other hand, he sees the theological and social dangers of homosexuality and fears the results of lifting the ban, as the Parliament of Great Britain did when it passed the Sex Offenses Act of 1967, permitting homosexual practices by consenting adults defined as anyone twenty-one years of age or older. Rodgers describes the results:

> Groups of active and militant gays have been allowed to address children in public schools. School children there have also been taken to a theatrical workshop in London to participate in something called the "Gay Sweatshop." Comprised of professional gay actors and using the facilities of a theater in Central London, the "Gay Sweatshop" puts on plays expressing the difficulties faced by homosexuals. The day-long program consists of two parts. In the morning the pupils are asked to participate in improvised plays, psycho dramas, and discussion groups centered around the theme of "feeling different." This is supposed to let the individual heterosexual youngster identify with the special condition of being homosexual; to let him or her feel the good points as well as the bad. In the afternoon, the pupils are treated to the professionally performed "entertainments" about homosexuality.[12]

[12]Rodgers, *The Gay Invasion,* p. 123.

Evangelical Christians, perhaps even more than other Americans, feel guilty and embarrassed when they are accused of violating the human rights of any group of people. Gays in European countries have succeeded in urging big name politicians to spend thousands of dollars in a mass media campaign to intimidate America into the same kind of acceptance of the gay community that most of those countries have adopted.

A classic example would be the *Time* magazine full-page advertisement in 1978 entitled "What's going on in America?" sponsored by the Foundation for Free Human Partnership in Amsterdam, The Netherlands. In addition to numerous Dutch celebrities, it was signed by a German theologian, several French authors including Jean-Paul Sartre, various Italian personalities, and the secretary of the International Council of Social Democratic Women of England. Here is a part of the message:

> In spite of the Declaration of Helsinki, in defense of which President Carter has declared himself so strongly abroad, in certain states homosexuals are excluded from government jobs. Many homosexuals have been denied housing, employment, and access to public accommodations.

> Max van der Stoel, the Dutch Minister of Foreign Affairs, justifiably stated that human rights are uprooted if they are not acknowledged without distinctions.

> We are alarmed by the campaign of Anita Bryant, who preaches discrimination in the name of God.

> We are also alarmed by the fact that many politi-

cians in America, who do not personally believe in discrimination against homosexuals, lack the courage to stand up to this bigotry. Some politicians have even jumped on the Bryant bandwagon of prejudice and injustice simply to further their own ambitions.

President Carter's human rights policy can gain credibility only if the rights of homosexuals in the United States of America are bound inseparably to human rights for all people. How can one advocate human rights to one's neighbor if one's own back yard is not in order?[13]

The intimidation is working, even in the evangelical community, as evidenced by a recent Harper and Row book, *Is the Homosexual My Neighbor,* authored by Christian feminists Letha Scanzoni and Virginia Mollenkott. Both of these ladies are brilliantly educated, articulate, and experienced authors. Their work is calm, reasonable, intelligent, and because of its pretense of being thoroughly biblical, it will unfortunately influence many.

Authors Scanzoni and Mollenkott accept the estimate that five to ten percent of the population is truly homosexual by fate, not by choice. While correctly debunking many of the myths about homosexuality that evangelicals have held in the past (many of which have also been treated with candor in this volume), they make the dangerous and patently unbiblical suggestion that Christians could consider encouraging homosexuals to enter into permanent loving relationships with chosen life partners of their own sex rather than failing at heterosexual marriage and wasting themselves in impersonal sexual en-

[13]*Time,* 16 January 1977, p. 74.

counters.[14] While attacking some myths, they accept others, such as the hackneyed gay claim that being homosexual is no more unusual than being left-handed. Evangelical theologians who questioned Scanzoni's feminist view of Scripture in an earlier volume (*All We're Meant to Be*, Word Books, 1975; co-authored with Nancy Hardesty) will have their suspicions confirmed upon reading *Is The Homosexual My Neighbor?* Although the book is a noble contribution to the growing literature on homosexuality because of the competence of the authors, it is destructive because of its mitigating and diluting attitude toward clear scriptural teaching.

Ostracism, obviously, is not the answer and it is not being advocated here. But the church is going to have to make a choice on the homosexual issue, and during the remainder of this century, we will see liberal churches, denominations, and perhaps even families being split over this growing social problem. The battle has just begun, and if history is any teacher (and it had better be), the trend will be toward a liberalizing of the church's viewpoint, precisely the same evolutionary process some evangelicals have adopted on the issues of divorce and adultery.

But since the emphasis should be on cure, rather than on accomodation, we should deal with a realistic story (utilizing a fictitious name) that shows the tremendous process that is sometimes necessary to bring about an effective cure of homosexuality. The story also reveals the dynamic and desperate need a former homosexual has for normal, God-designed relations with a member of the opposite sex.

[14]*Is the Homosexual My Neighbor? Another Christian View* (New York: Harper & Row, 1978).

Billy was an arsonist, and it is not uncommon to find some kind of sexual deviation linked with arson in a tangled life like Billy's. His homosexuality was not discovered until after his incarceration for arson, but there are few secrets behind prison walls and Billy's homosexual practice began to take on a pronounced new impetus.

In prison he met Jesus Christ and understood that while he himself was atoning for his crimes, only the Son of God could atone for his sin, and so both sin and crime were behind him when he went out on bail in the mid-1970s.

Excited about his new faith and wanting to learn more of the Word of God, Billy enrolled in a Bible school and seemed to be making satisfactory progress until one day he left everything behind—billfold, Bible, clothes, personal belongings—and started wandering again into the free-wheeling life-style he had known before his arson conviction and subsequent imprisonment. But he never returned to his homosexuality, and in the gracious providence of God, Billy wound up with his grandparents in Ohio and received legal permission to stay there without recrimination for jumping bail in another state.

Recently, Billy married a younger girl who previously had given birth to a baby out of wedlock, and he is genuinely trying to make a new life for all of them. Hardly a solid start for a happy family, you say? True, but those whose lives are shattered by sexual sin have to begin again where Christ transforms them. They do not have the opportunity of creating a fictitious, idealistic past.

One of the repetitious themes in Billy's letters to his former chaplain and continuing friend is the desperate loneliness that brought him to marriage. He needed to prove to himself and to society that a "transformed homosexual" could relate positively to a wife and child.

It is too early to say whether Billy and his new wife will become a model Christian family, but we certainly can learn from his story the tremendous need of a former homosexual to enter as soon as possible into a normal relationship with a member of the opposite sex—to see whether or not he or she can really establish a healthy marriage.

CHAPTER 11

THE HOMOSEXUAL AND THE CHURCH

In assessing "the evangelical mood at the end of 1977" William J. Peterson identified several "big issues." He talked about the charismatic movement, relations between Roman Catholics and Protestants, the women's movement, and the gay question.

> Homosexuality will remain a hot issue, but it is doubtful there will be a change in evangelical outlook. However, homosexuality will be brought out of the evangelical closet as the church is forced to find a way to minister to homosexuals, in the same way it has been forced to minister to divorcees.[1]

This chapter is not primarily geared to an analysis of homosexual churches. Obviously, homosexuals have a legal right to establish churches just as does any other cult, and they have already begun to exercise that right in great numbers. The "mother congregation," San Francisco's Metropolitan Church, continues to plan great growth. Troy Perry, its

[1]"The Evangelical Mood at the End of 1977," *Evangelical Newsletter*, vol. 4, no. 24 (2 December 1977): 4.

founder and the moderator of the Universal Fellow ship of Metropolitan Community Churches, claimed in 1977 that there were 103 congregations in 7 countries with a total membership of 20,731.[2]

The concern here is with the reaction of established evangelical churches. Is there some balanced and biblical position between the excesses of unreasoning bitterness on one hand and unthinking acceptance on the other? I think there is and I think it is characterized by an approach that should be welcomed both by Bible-believing Christian leaders and by serious homosexuals who recognize their problem and are seeking a solution honestly.

At the time this book was being edited the General Assembly of the United Presbyterian church voted against accepting a recommendation of a special task force which had advised the denomination to proceed with the ordination of gays. To illustrate how seriously the "gay Christian" viewpoint is being considered in some denominations, here are some of the conclusions the task force urged (unsuccessfully) the United Presbyterians to accept.

> Sexual orientation is best understood as affectional attraction rather than sexual behavior, and homosexuality "is a strong, enduring, not consciously chosen and usually irreversible affectional attraction to and preference for persons of the same sex."

> Homosexuality is "a minor theme in Scripture" and is not mentioned either by the prophets or by Jesus himself.

[2]"Homosexual Ordination: Bishops Feel the Flack," *Christianity Today* (4 March 1977): 51.

In the full context of Scripture, ". . . we must conclude that Paul's understanding of homosexual behavior does not adequately encompass the modern phenomenon of multiple forms of homosexuality arising from a variety of psychosocial causes. . . ."

Homosexuals may be admitted to church membership or the ordained offices if they can give honest affirmation to the vows required and if the deciding body is satisfied that the candidates meet all the criteria for membership or ordination. (Deacons and ruling elders in UPC churches are ordained and take nearly the same vows as the clergy.)

Nothing in the church's constitution either prohibits or requires the ordination of avowed homosexuals; the judgment of the ordaining body as to fitness of any candidate—judged as an individual—is the decisive factor.

Ordination does not set a person apart "into a class or status separated from other Christians."

Continuing and widespread study is needed, including efforts to heal the church of its "homophobia," described as the irrational fear of homosexuality and homosexuals.[3]

If the General Assembly would have ratified that recommendation, most likely a general brouhaha would have developed similar to what happened in the Episcopal church earlier. But chances are it would have been much more divisive since there are many more conservative congregations in the United

[3]"United Presbyterians: Bracing for Battle," *Christianity Today* (10 February 1978): 48.

Presbyterian church than in the Episcopal church.

Without question the gay issue is going to be continually divisive, and I'm not sure that Peterson is right when he says that evangelicals won't change their position. I believe evangelicals will fight about the issue of whether or not homosexuals should be "accepted" in the established church. And, if so, under what terms, toward what end, and at what risk?

The novelist Morris West put the following words into the mouth of one of his characters in *The Devil's Advocate*. The character was the homosexual painter Nicholas Black.

> Let's say I am what everybody calls me—an unnatural man, a corrupter of youth. What does the Church offer me by way of faith, hope, or charity? . . . do I need love the less? Do I need satisfaction less? Have I less right to live in contentment because somewhere along the line the Almighty slipped a cog in creation?[4]

To be sure, West is a Catholic novelist and he speaks about his own church. Furthermore, he makes Nicholas Black utter the old line about homosexuality being genetic. But he has a point. What does the church have to offer the homosexual?

In many cases there has been no openness at all on the part of the evangelical community to minister to the homosexual. Perhaps the problem is not so much a lack of compassion, but rather a gross misunderstanding aided by the repulsive behavior of militant gays and the tendency of some religiously oriented

[4]*The Devil's Advocate* (New York: William Morrow, 1959), pp. 257, 259.

homosexuals to gravitate toward their own religious experience, as in the Metropolitan Church.

Anita Bryant has been much maligned (for the most part unjustly) for her stand against providing special privileges for homosexuals and laws that protect their behavior. I believe she is entirely right when she expresses her own genuine love for repentant homosexuals and an open admission that the evangelical community has fumbled the ball on the issue.

> I have a dream of setting up centers across the country, because an awful lot of people have been turned off by the church. I mean the word homosexual hasn't even been heard in the church—homosexuality has been a taboo. The church has failed miserably in this respect. Homosexuality being brought into the open is a good thing because it gives Christians an opportunity in love to share that there is hope for the homosexual. . . . Really what homosexuals are searching for is just to be needed and wanted and loved, but unfortunately this need manifests itself in lust rather than love and that is the beguilement of the Devil in the homosexual community.[5]

Anita tells the story of a young boy who wrote to apologize for the vicious attacks she has experienced from the homosexual community. He then explained, "I was born a homosexual." After initial contact by phone and letter, one of the workers from the Save our Children movement went by and led the young man to the Lord. But when homosexuals ac-

[5] "Door Interview: Anita Bryant," *Wittenburg Door*, no. 39 (October–November 1977): 12.

cept Christ they are like other new converts whose lives have been plagued by some kind of physical sin. Yes, occasionally God does immediately change an alcoholic so that he never touches another drink. More than likely, however, alcoholism, smoking, masturbation, and homosexuality—behaviors which are grounded in habituation—tend to hang on and reappear again and again.

The young man in Miami (we'll call him John) was a typical case. Even after he trusted Christ the pressures were enormous and backsliding was a pattern of life because of the addictive grip homosexuality had upon him.

John's childhood had been extremely unfortunate. His parents were alcoholics; his uncle was a homosexual; his friends scoffed at him for his attempts at a Christian life-style. John was an example of a homosexual who desperately needed acceptance by the evangelical church. But where could he go? What congregation would understand? Should he explain his past? John's frustrations mounted because of the vacuum of understanding and ministry to repentant homosexuals.

The key is the attitude of the homosexual toward the sin question. If the practice of homosexuality is a sin, and if homosexuals accept it as such, then churches need to accept homosexuals as repentant sinners. This is, of course, not to accept homosexuality as normal, but it also means that we do not condemn the *person* because of the *propensity*. Quite obviously, no thinking evangelical could go along with modern liberals like Union Seminary's John P. Rash who doubts that the Bible condemns homosexuality in general but merely the perverse cultivation of it. Nevertheless, some clergymen are certainly correct when they complain that the churches themselves have sinned by omission when they fail to speak out against harassment and debasement of homosexuals.[6]

As a conservative Christian I take no pride in a letter such as the one Ralph Blair claims he received from the vice president and general supervisor of one evangelical denomination in response to an inquiry regarding that church's position on homosexuality.

> Our position is that it is a vicious, dirty, and unscriptural, cancerous blight on humanity. Any . . . person . . . within our church is subject to immediate dismissal if it is known and proven that the (sic) are participating in this degrading practice. We have no time, place, or sympathy with it or for it in any degree, whatsoever.[7]

I would agree with this statement if it concerned blatant, overt, militant gayism. But there certainly needs to be an acceptance of the repentant homosexual who comes to a biblical awareness of his sin.

Note the preferable attitude demonstrated in an editorial in *Christianity Today*.

> Unfortunately, the Christian church has not shown any great ability to accept them either, or to help them. And for that we are partially to blame. Acceptance cannot mean acceptance of the homosexual's views, as many of the clergy are now doing, but it must mean acceptance of the deviate as a person for whom Christ died and for whom the Gospel holds transforming hope.
>
> Christians have nothing to offer if they regard the homosexual as an untouchable, a sinner beyond

[6]"The Gay Church, *Time*, 23 August 1971, p. 39.
[7]Blair, "Evangelical Look at Homosexuality": 2.

the sphere of their concern. But they do him a disservice if they settle for less than the full biblical teaching about sex. Compassion for the deviate must involve God's standards. It must also involve the promise of a power beyond ourselves, the power that is able to lead men into the full enjoyment of the nature that God gave them.[8]

Repentance

Partly at fault here is a weak view of repentance Without lapsing into the interesting but probably futile argument about "Lordship salvation," let me affirm as clearly as I can that repentance surely has two sides. The word *metanola* does not mean to weep profusely and beat one's chest in sorrow, but it does mean to turn and go the other way. And when one turns, he must turn "from" as well as "to." An "easy-believism" (to borrow a phrase from A. W. Tozer), which tells the homosexual that he can become a Christian and continue to practice his homosexuality—to affirm his inner self as a legitimate life-style, is a distortion of the gospel and a renunciation of the regenerating work of the Holy Spirit.

To compare a homosexual with the woman taken in adultery (John 8) is no major problem as long as we are willing to look at the whole story. Those who would advance the cause of gay militancy, however, pick out phrases like "Let him who is without sin among you be the first to throw a stone at her" and "Neither do I condemn thee," but conveniently forget the parting command of Jesus, "Go, and sin no more."

[8]"The Bible and the Homosexual," *Christianity Today* (19 January 1968): 25.

But aren't all men sinful? And does not the Bible teach that all are equally redeemable? Harold Lindsell answers both questions:

It is quite true that all men are sinful. It is also true that all men are redeemable. But the redemption of men does more than secure their acceptance by God and supply them with the grace of justification. They are also delivered from sin's thralldom. No one can be justified who does not repent. And repentance includes a turning from the old life and the old sins.[9]

Well, can a homosexual be a Christian or not? Evangelical "authorities" are quite divided on that question. William Standish Reed says, "It is my opinion from Scripture that there is no such thing as a Christian homosexual. We would not consider a minister of the gospel to be proper were he to keep a mistress. Therefore, how could we consider him to be proper if he has homosexual activities?"[10] But Richard Lovelace, professor of church history at Gordon-Conwell Theological Seminary, holds an obviously different view in his discussion of the valuable ministry that "gay believers" can perform in behalf of the evangelical community.

Christians should call for a substantial recovery of uncloseted gay believers striving for continence and recommend this lifestyle to the gay community because it has already been demonstrated that God can use these men and women very powerfully in reaching and ministering to

[9]"Homosexuals and the Church," *Christianity Today* (28 September 1973): 12.
[10]"The Homosexual: Does He Belong in the Church?" *Christian Life* (October 1967): 67.

gays. Gay believers have performed a service in exposing and breaking through our homophobia and neglect of this field of nurture and evangelism. The church's sponsorship of openly avowed, repentant homosexuals in leadership positions would not only be effective in attracting other gays, but it would also say something profound about the power of the Gospel to free the church from homophobia and the homosexual from guilt and bondage.[11]

As usual, the truth probably lies somewhere between these two diverse positions. Quite obviously there can be homosexual Christians because there are. By the same token, Lovelace stops short of the real power of the gospel when he wants it used only to "free the church from homophobia and the homosexual from guilt and bondage." If homosexuality is not genetic, if it is primarily psychological and based on habituated behavior patterns, if it is sin as well as sickness, then the sin can be forgiven and the sickness cured. So the homosexual is freed not only from "guilt and bondage" but also from the grip of his physical life patterns. Charles Young sums up this issue well:

Certainly I believe a person with a homosexual problem can become a Christian. Christ does not insist that we have all our problems solved or our personalities tidied up before we ask for forgiveness and renewal of life. I am equally sure that a person repeatedly committing homosexual acts cannot be a maturing, witnessing Christian for the following reasons: When a person commits

[11]"How Evangelicals Should Respond to the Homosexual Issue," *Evangelical Newsletter,* vol. 4, no. 9 (23 September 1977): 4.

himself to Christ, he expresses a willingness to change his ways. If the person continues to practice acts which are explicitly forbidden by Scripture, and which may injure or destroy another individual, we wonder about his willingness to cooperate with God who helps those who are willing and want to be helped.[12]

We shall talk more about cure in the next chapter, but the road to cure must be built upon a love that offers hope.

Love

Closely akin to acceptance is love. But though it is closely akin, love is evidence of a concern that goes deeper. Can you love a person who has been sexually immoral and is now repentant? Can you love a person who was involved with idolatry and now wants to turn to Christ? Can you love a former adulterer, thief, greedy person, drunk, gossip, or swindler? Of course! This is precisely what the gospel is all about, and the gospel is for the gay too. The point is, of course, that the sickness and sin must be recognized and repentance must be apparent, along with faith to believe that God can change the homosexual's life and life-style. Lindsell spells it out clearly:

No human being invented the Christian faith. It was God's idea. If you think it a bad idea, you'd better blame God. . . . He gave us this Christianity. We can accept it. We can reject it. But we can't tamper with it as though it were something put together by human hands or human brains. . . . The final and conclusive argument against

[12]"Homosexuality and the Campus," *HIS* (February 1966): 15.

homosexuality does not come from the psychologists, the sociologists, the secularists, or the humanists. It comes from God, who has spoken His Word against it and has never stuttered in His speech.[13]

Hope

While the Scripture explicitly denounces homosexual behavior, it also announces hope for the believer. The glorious proclamation of 1 Corinthians 6:9-11 is the biblical affirmation that homosexuals can be changed—there is simply no other acceptable interpretation of the passage. Indeed, it is so clear that this proclamation of hope must be ignored by "gay evangelicals" who wish to proclaim a "practicing" viewpoint.

Yes, homosexual behavior is a sin and God hates sin. But God also forgives sin and changes the sinner. A genuine proclamation of hope, forgiveness, and renewal shows again that the truth is relevant to the issues of any generation. The beautiful balance of the Bible must be adopted by those who wish to proclaim it. Condemnation is balanced by forgiveness and the homosexual must experience the love of God and the love of His people. To be sure, homosexuality is not a sin greater than all others, nor is it any more difficult to receive forgiveness if one has been a practicing gay. Emotional rebirth may be a slow process, much like rehabilitation, but that does not say that God's grace is not working in the life.

Burl DeLong notes that "the fact that many gay pastors and parishioners come from fundamentalistic backgrounds strongly suggests that the church has failed to minister to the homosexual. This may be a

[13]"Homosexuals and the Church": 12.

major cause for the emergence of the gay church and the confrontation now taking place between the church and the homosexual community.[14]

Perhaps this chapter on the response of the church to the homosexual can best be terminated by the description of what one church is doing. Brookvalley Church in Atlanta, Georgia, discovered that it "was sitting on the commercial crossroads of the gay business world and the gay residential community." In conjunction with WHAE-TV, the Atlanta Christian Broadcasting Network affiliate, Pastor Jim Bevis organized a conference providing training toward "ministering to the homosexual from a biblical basis." Bevis would be the first to say that the church hasn't found all the answers nor has it yet done all it hopes to do in its ministry to homosexuals. But as he puts it, "we have taken the first step—we have become informed, ready to be counselors who have a better, more loving and compassionate perspective on the problem. The conference has laid the groundwork; we at Brookvalley are waiting to see in what new direction God will lead us."[15]

[14]"A Critique of Current Evangelical Interpretation Regarding the Biblical Understanding of Homosexuality" (Master's Degree thesis, Dallas Theological Seminary, 1977), p. 50.

[15]"How One Church Handles Homosexuals," *Christian Life* (November 1977): 24–25, 58.

CHAPTER 12

TAKING THE CURE

Jim Dolby, a former high school classmate of mine who has a doctorate in psychology and is now a professional counselor, tells the story of a young man he calls John. John first sought help with his homosexual problem after reading an article telling how homosexuals could be changed. When confronted with the young man's question, "Is there anything that can be done to help?" Dolby told him that many persons had been able to resolve their problems to the point where they could live normal, heterosexual lives. An obvious sense of relief settled over the young college sophomore. After a year of psychotherapeutic counseling, John's life was changed and he is now husband of a lovely wife and father of a normal and happy daughter.

What made the difference? From John's point of view it was an eagerness to change, a faith in Christ, and a willingness to recognize the distortion of his life. He did not passively accept his "fate," a tremendous hindrance to homosexual change brought about by widespread belief in the genetic-cause theory.

But the love and understanding of his counselor was also a key. Rather than being judgmental or

162

insisting upon immediate change, Dolby carefully helped John work through his problem until he could understand himself and recognize how Christ could change him.

To be sure, we are not all trained psychotherapists with appropriate training and time to offer help to people suffering from sexual deviations, but Dolby suggests what we can do.

> The counselee needs to know that God understands all man's human frailties and cares beyond measure. Often, guilt is an integral part of this neurosis, and the pastor should meet this with a spirit of understanding and forgiveness, symbolizing God's grace on man's behalf.[1]

Christians need to be more faithful in offering the homosexual the hope we surely agree God offers. The following quotes are excerpted from letters written by former homosexuals to Anita Bryant. Each indicates the power of God in setting captive homosexuals free.

> Jesus came into my life about a year and a half ago. I was gay. . . . The only true gay liberation is believing that Jesus is Lord, and in repentance from the abominable sin of homosexuality.

> I am a 27-year-old man who has been set free of homosexuality by the power and love of Jesus Christ.
>
> I know what a false life, a lonely life that gay life is. All I ever wanted was true love. I never found it through lovers, but I found it when I allowed Jesus to be Lord of my life. . . .

[1]"Helping the Homosexual," *Christianity Today* (16 February 1968): 29–30.

> Dec. 25 was a turning point in my life, as the Holy Spirit directed me to stand before a packed church and give my testimony of how Jesus had set me free of being a homosexual. . . .

> I write to tell you of one more homosexual redeemed by Christ, namely myself. I was actively involved in the gay movement at my university. I had sincere, passionate love for my lesbian sisters. . . .
> Well, the Lord changed my way of life. God desires so much to see adversary militant homosexuals repent of their sin, just as I have done. . . .[2]

Surely, the evidence suggests that homosexuals can be "cured." Many words could be used synonymously here—"liberated," "delivered," "healed" —but perhaps the simplest and most poignant word is *cure*. Interestingly enough, any of these words can be used both for sin and sickness. The Bible speaks of healing in both the spiritual and physical senses, and as I have been trying to emphasize, both are applicable to the homosexual. Charles Young's thought-provoking article on helping homosexuals, based on analysis of a number of studies, ends on a most encouraging note: "From my own clinical experience in dealing with homosexuals, I believe there is solid ground for optimism for them. For the person who has not given himself over to homosexuality and who desires help, I believe there is real hope."[3]

And again, "The Christian group can offer reasonable hope and encouragement to the homosexual

[2]*The Miami Herald,* 29 January 1978, p. 2G.
[3]Young, "Homosexuality and the Campus": 23.

who desires to change his ways. It can challenge him to identify and use his latent powers, and to utilize the available spiritual and scientific resources in his redemption."[4]

Klaus Bockmühl cites a fifty percent cure rate of homosexuals in the New York Academy of Medical Science Psychiatric Division.[5] But the problem is to convince the overt homosexual to begin treatment. A climate of permissiveness with an emphasis on "civil rights legislation" is opposed to the best interests of homosexuals who can receive both healing from the sickness and forgiveness from the sin that characterizes their perversion.

It would seem that four ingredients are essential if the church is to offer any kind of cure to homosexuals.

1. Recognition That Homosexuality Is Not Genetically Caused

Constitutional theories explaining the cause of homosexuality have been the greatest deterrent to solving the problem. Dr. Stanley H. Mullen writes:

> If a person is born without gonadol function, he is without sexual inclination in any direction. That preponderance of estrogens or a relative lack of androgens has anything at all to do with male homosexual activity has been rather conclusively negatively demonstrated by William H. Perloff in an article on "Hormones and Homosexuality" published in a book edited by Judd Marmor: *Sexual Inversion: The Multiple Roots of Homosexuality*. Perloff concludes by

[4]Ibid.: 24.
[5]"Homosexuality and Biblical Perspective," *Christianity Today* (16 February 1973): 17.

stating "Homosexuality is a purely psychological phenomenon, neither dependent on a hormonal pattern for its production nor amenable to change by endocrine substances." Note that saying homosexuality is a "purely psychological phenomenon" does *not* rule out the fact that religious factors may still have a significant bearing on the problem; for *choices* are based on ethical and religious considerations, and these *do* have considerable effect on the *psyche's* formation.[6]

2. Repentance on the Part of the Homosexual

Jesus asked, "Wilt thou be made whole?" To such a question, which the Savior still asks today, the homosexual sincerely desiring help must admit the sin of his past life, repent, accept forgiveness, and begin the struggle against his old nature, which will be driving him toward the practice of homosexuality. To be sure, a call for repentance flies in the face of contemporary permissiveness in Western culture. But the Law is the agent to drive us to grace, and unless we recognize homosexuality for what it is, we will always go along excusing the behavior and thereby offering no hope for change. Again Bock mühl lays it on the line.

The Church of Jesus Christ has to resist the trend that would ironically make it the agent for the abolition of its own ethical norms, an abolition for which neither the Old nor the New Testament offers the slightest justification. The biblical norms are relevant precisely because they deal with homosexual *behavior,* which is exactly the problem today. It is impossible to see why the

[6]"The Homosexual, Does He Belong in the Church?": 39

principle of the lordship of Christ, which is applicable to every other aspect of human shortcoming and error, should not also have a healing and helpful impact in the area of homosexuality.[7]

3. Responsible Counseling By Competent Christians

The Christian who wishes to put his acceptance and love into action may want to get involved with counseling the homosexual. If Dr. Larry Crabb is right and the evangelical congregation is the best context for Christian counseling, then the needs of the homosexual cannot be considered any less important than those of any other person whose psychological or physiological make-up make him a candidate for Christian counseling. However, when a particular case is beyond our ability to be of genuine help, then referral to a professional is in order.

Howard A. Eyrich notes "the capitulation of liberal Christianity" and "the confusion of conservative Christianity" in dealing with the complex issues of homosexuality. He then proceeds to suggest how the Jay Adams's brand of "nouthetic counseling" would approach the problem. To be sure, nouthetic counseling is only one approach acceptable among evangelical psychologists. But it does offer a proposal for treatment based upon three presuppositions that have already been affirmed in this book: The absoluteness of the Word of God; the fact that homosexuality is sin; and the assumption that homosexuality is a learned behavior.

When implementing the nouthetic technique we have already talked about the counseling procedures that Eyrich calls "establishing hope" and "bridge

[7]"Bockmühl, Homosexuality and Biblical Perspective": 17–18.

burning.'' The third element in the nouthetic cure requires further examination at this point. Because Adams assumes (probably with accuracy) that homosexuality interpenetrates and affects every area of life, the nouthetic approach must *restructure* the entire life attempting to bring it into conformity to biblical patterns. Eyrich quotes from Adams concerning the approach.

> To counsel homosexuals, counselors must get a commitment for total *structuring*. It is not only those who have lived a life of general irresponsibility who need structuring. Whenever a counselee's problem turns out to be one large, glaring sin like homosexuality, he may believe, wrongly, that he has only one problem to solve. . . . But in such cases *the* problem cannot help but affect every other aspect of his life, work, physical and financial matters, etc. All these areas must be investigated and restructured biblically. . . . If counseling focuses upon only the issue of homosexuality usually it will fail . . . unless he shores up each of the areas of his life before God, they will constantly tend to drag him back toward homosexual sin in spite of good intentions. The counselee, therefore, must be shown the importance of total structuring and must be urged to work hard in each area of his life by the power of the Spirit.[8]

It is not my purpose to recommend Adams's nouthetic approach above Dolby's psychotherapy or Crabb's congregational acceptance. The point is that

[8]Quoted from *The Journal of Pastoral Practice,* vol. 1, no. 2 (Summer 1977): 31. The quote is taken from J. E. Adams, *The Christian Counselor's Manual* (Nutley, N.J.: Presbyterian and Reformed Pub. Co., 1973), pp. 409–11.

homosexuals can be counseled, they can be helped, and they can be cured.

4. Receptive Christians Who Practice Acceptance and Love

It should be clear by this point that I am committed to the absolute nature of biblical teaching on homosexuality and strongly believe that the church does itself and the homosexual a grave disservice if it settles for less than what the Bible has to say and how the Bible has to say it. It is not an act of compassion in the name of love or acceptance to abolish biblical standards for the sake of any individual.

But Christians have nothing to offer if they regard the homosexual as untouchable and totally beyond help and love. They are also of no use to him if unwilling to at least attempt to lead him to the cure discussed in this chapter. God uses the body of Christ to change people. The church is not made up of good people, but bad people who have been changed by the power of God.

A short time ago my friend, John MacArthur, pastor of the Grace Community Church in Panorama City, California, was involved in a "round table discussion" on the subject of homosexuality sponsored by *Inspiration* magazine. The magazine report of the discussion includes MacArthur's summary, an argument that I have tried to make repeatedly throughout the pages of this book. MacArthur forced the issue back to the basis of authority and raised the same question I did at the beginning of this study—"Do you believe the Bible?" In approaching the homosexual problem on the basis of the frequent illustrations in Scripture comparing Christ and the church to a husband-wife relationship, MacArthur tied down the argument with these words:

> The assumption is never made that any other kind of relationship would ever enter into a position of leadership in the church of Christ . . . that any other kind of relationship would ever be a model for any definition of the Church. And from that standpoint, I feel that what we have here is an obtuse kind of behavior that is being tolerated today and then intellectualized today and then imposed upon the Word of God—and the sad thing in all of this, the thing that really grieves my heart, is that we are denying the cure because we are denying the sin.[9]

[9]"An Historic Dialogue . . . Homosexuality: A Gift From God?" *Inspiration* (March–April, 1978): 112.

APPENDIX 1

A Critical Review:

HOMOSEXUALITY IN THE WESTERN CHRISTIAN TRADITION

BY DERRICK SHERWIN BAILEY

This scholarly and definitive work was first published in 1955. No evangelical scholar dealing with the subject of homosexuality has done his homework without thoroughly grappling with Bailey's arguments.

In the introduction to his book Bailey clearly states his goal: "My object has been simply to state as accurately and to examine as fully as possible the biblical and ecclesiastical attitudes to homosexual practice, and the contributions of Roman Law and medieval thought to the views which are now current in the West." But in the very next paragraph he states, "Since this is mainly an historical study, I have refrained from any discussion of the theological and moral aspects of homosexuality, and of the morality of homosexual acts between males in particular."

So the warning even weaves its way through the introduction, much less in the text of the book. Bailey is faced with the question of how it is possible "to examine as fully as possible" biblical attitudes on homosexuality without discussing "the theological and moral aspects of homosexuality." If a thorough biblical exegesis of all related passages is not the foundation for our Christian understanding of theological and moral aspects, what is?

Such is precisely the essential weakness in Bailey's treatment and he has been honest enough to warn us right in the title. His concern and thesis is based on the understanding of homosexuality in *"the Western Christian tradition,"* not in the biblical text itself.

Consequently, the biblical treatment of the Sodom and Gomorrah story receives about sixteen pages; all other "definite references" including all Pauline passages approximately twelve pages; and "possible references" about five pages. Bailey's "summary of biblical evidence" is laid to rest on page 61 of a 176 page monograph with the following sentence:

> In any final assessment, the development of this attitude cannot be considered apart from the process of reinterpretation by which the Sodom story acquired its homosexual significance, with the consequence that the fate of the city came to symbolize the retribution awaiting both those who indulge in the vice which is supposed to have been its downfall, and the society which condones such depravity of conduct.[1]

The rest of the book deals with rabbinical thought, pre-Constantinian legislation and practice, the attitudes and edicts of the Christian emperors, Patristic thought, enactments of councils and synods, the penitentials, medieval opinion, Aristotilian studies, Heriten and Bougre, and finally, the law in England. In short, Bailey's book is a most helpful history of attitudes and laws on homosexuality in Western cul-

[1]D. Sherwin Bailey, *Homosexuality and the Western Christian Tradition* (New York: Longmans, 1955).

ture, but as any kind of a biblical treatise it is an abject failure.

Furthermore, it is completely unacceptable to evangelicals for several reasons that make themselves quite obvious in a careful study of the author's arguments. His refusal to recognize *yoda* as dealing with sexual behavior in the Sodom account may be understandable and even forgivable, though it certainly is in opposition to all orthodox scholarship of almost two thousand years of church history. The argument, however, is so absolutely essential to a gay treatment of the Sodom account that we must expect Bailey to cling tenaciously to it.

What we dare not accept, however, is his loose treatment of the doctrine of inspiration that he uses to apply the *theory of accommodation* to the biblical account of the destruction of Sodom and Gomorrah.

> So sudden and complete a devastation of these prosperous cities [a destruction which Bailey considers to be exclusively caused by natural phenomena] would create an indelible impression upon the people of that time who, being ignorant of the scientific explanation, would inevitably tend to ascribe the disaster to supernatural agencies. In this way, no doubt, began the theory of a Divine visitation and judgment for sin, which developed into the familiar Sodom story of the Bible.[2]

But the ignorant Old Testament characters who completely misunderstood the Sodom account were also victims of another problem, namely, the *folklore of the surrounding peoples* whose legends tell how strangers frequently visited a city where they were

[2]Ibid., p. 7.

refused hospitality and the cities would eventually meet some kind of disaster. The evangelical reader asks immediately, "Why could not the folklore of surrounding peoples have taken their cue from the actual historical account of Sodom and Gomorrah rather than the biblical account being constructed from pagan mythology?" Excellent question, and one answered by the simple fact that Bailey accepts without question the *documentary hypothesis of the authorship of the Pentateuch.*

> And if the tale of the natural disaster which over-threw the cities of the Plain was gradually moulded by subconscious influences into yet another version of the basic myth which has just been described, then a further point of some sig-nificance emerges. In the legends, as in the Yahwist's narrative in Genesis xix, the conduct which brings judgment upon the offending com-munity and leads to its destruction is never sex-ual, but always wickedness in general, and in particular, inhospitality. This, again, suggests that the association of homosexual practices with the Sodom story is a late and extrinsic feature which, for some reason, has been read into the original account.[3]

And so not only the apostle Paul, but also Peter and Jude were victims of this gradually developing mythological interpretation of the Sodom account. Rather than being guided by the Holy Spirit to record inspired, inerrant, authoritative accounts of the de-struction of Sodom and God's attitude toward homosexual practice, the New Testament authors picked up their hermeneutic from apocryphal litera-ture.

[3]Ibid., p. 8.

If this inference is substantially correct, it enables us to locate the source of the Christian interpretation of the Sodom story, and also to account for the marked similarity of thought and idiom displayed by the passages relating to Sodom in the book of *Jubilees,* and the testament of *Naphtali*—a similarity which is clearly to be explained by the common theory underlying them.[4]

The greatest influence on the thought of New Testament writers was the *Hellenistic interpretation set forth by Philo and Josephus.* According to Bailey, "The traditional Christian opinion that the Sodomites were annihilated because of their homosexual practices can be traced to its origin and a conception of the sin of Sodom which appeared first in Palestine during the second century B.C." If one has no concern for the Holy Spirit's control of the minds and hearts of New Testament writers, one could be disposed to argue with Bailey:

. . . There is not the least reason to believe, as a matter of either historical fact or of revealed truth, that the city of Sodom and its neighbours were destroyed because of their homosexual practices. This theory of their fate seems undoubtedly to have originated in a Palestinian Jewish reinterpretation of Genesis xix inspired by antagonism to the Hellenistic way of life and its exponents, and by contempt for the basest features of Greek sexual immorality.[5]

So much for Sodom, but what about the Levitical passages? As long as one clings to the JEPD theory

[4]Ibid., pp. 17–18.
[5]Ibid., p. 27.

and assumes a late date of the Pentateuch, he can attribute all of it to a *gradual growth of the mythological concept.* So Bailey says:

> These laws cannot be accurately dated, so we do not know whether they reflect an early or a late attitude to homosexual practices; moreover, it is difficult to say whether they were dictated by the exigencies of some particular social situation, or whether they are simply items of abstract legislation designed to provide against a future possible occurrence of the offenses penalized.[6]

Though the evangelical scholar will find Bailey's conclusions unacceptable because of his premises, the carefulness of Bailey's scholarship will generally be respected. But at various points one wonders what sources Bailey used. For example, what could possibly be the basis for his statement that "there is no reason to suppose that unnatural practices were so markedly characteristic of the nations which surrounded Israel that they specially endangered Hebrew morals."[7] The inseparability of pagan idolatry and sexual immorality has already been documented in the early chapters of this book.

It is almost superfluous to mention Bailey's treatment of the Gibeah account in Judges 19 since it stems again from the same documentary hypothesis that colors his entire treatment of Scripture. The text of Judges 19 is simply not reliable because "it is the result of a process of recension during which (as even a casual perusal of the narrative will show) the Gibeah story was extensively and, it seems, deliber-

[6]Ibid., p. 29.
[7]Ibid., p. 37.

ately assimilated to the Sodom story" and "the narrative in its extant form has obviously been edited."[8] When in doubt, argue *textual corruption*—as long as your conscience is not troubled by the doctrine of biblical inspiration!

One more comment on Bailey's work. As a typical modern liberal scholar, he falls prey to the *existential pitfall of relativism* and therefore concludes:

> It is no longer permissible to take refuge in the contention that God Himself pronounced these acts "detestable and abominable" above every other sexual sin, nor to explain natural catastrophes and human disasters as His vengeance upon those who indulge in them. It is much to be hoped that we shall soon hear the last of Sodom and Gomorrah in connection with homosexual practices—though doubtless the term "sodomy" will always remain as a reminder of the unfortunate consequences which have attended the reinterpretation of an ancient story in the interest of propaganda.[9]

Let me affirm again the importance to the evangelical Christian of a careful study of Bailey's work. It demonstrates clearly the basis for the false hope held out to self-declared "gay evangelicals" like Ralph Blair and shows clearly that an evangelical doctrine of inspiration cannot be made compatible with the gay exegesis of the biblical texts related to homosexuality. But it also has a most interesting list of the "positive features" of the Christian tradition in which Bailey correctly reminds us "that the

[8]Ibid., p. 53.
[9]Ibid., p. 155.

homosexual offender is not only a criminal who may deserve punishment, but also a sinner who needs to be won to repentance; and that justice must therefore be tempered with mercy."[10]

[10]Ibid., p. 174.

Appendix 2

ONE MINUTE AND FORTY-EIGHT SECONDS ON HOMOSEXUALITY

On November 17, 1971, Los Angeles radio station KABC offered "a solid twenty-four hours" of discussion on homosexuality. The director of the station aired an editorial in which he urged the California State Legislature to pass a bill to permit "consenting adults" to practice homosexuality privately (note how mild that proposal is when compared with the repealed Miami Metro Ordinance). The editorial, of course, required equal time for reply, and in one minute and forty-eight seconds, Dr. Paul Popenoe of the American Institute of Family Relations offered the following address:

Homosexuality, said a committee of the New York Academy of Medicine, is "an illness of social proportion, national significance, and serious portent." It is usually found in civilizations that are decaying and approaching disintegration. In no such nation, to my knowledge, has it been promoted so aggressively as in ours at the present time. Viscount Hailsham, in his report to the British government, called it "a proselytizing religion." It can exist only by continually recruiting new victims. Sociologist Judson T. Landis of the University in Berkeley questioned eighteen hundred college students; more than five hundred said they had been approached by homosexuals, two-thirds of them when they were not more than sixteen years old. Dr. Evelyn Hooker of UCLA, after investigations in Los Angeles, spoke of the "frantic promiscuity" of the homosexual community here. Says the distinguished Canadian authority, Dr. Daniel Cappon, "the natural history of the homosexual person seems to be one of frigidity, impotence, broken personal relationships, psycho-somatic disorders, alcoholism, paranoid psychosis, and suicide." It is thoroughly demonstrated that any homosexual can be changed if he wants to be. No one had to become a homosexual. No one has to remain a homosexual. There is no more reason to allow such persons to continue dragging new victims into their miserable existence, than to allow a person sick with any other serious communicable disease to spread his illness to the public. If it spreads, homosexuality must inevitably end in the extermination of the race that practices it. California should work resolutely toward a culture that is life oriented, not death oriented.

APPENDIX 3

HELPING THE HOMOSEXUAL: ONE WOMAN'S EXPERIENCE

Susan was a young Christian who had enjoyed a beautiful childhood and adolescence in a Christian family. She had no deep-seated emotional problems and was apparently a young adult quite at peace with herself and the world, well-adjusted, and in good psychological health.

But Susan had one important blind spot—she was totally unaware of the implications of a female friendship that expressed itself in physical behaviors. But let's let her tell her own story.

The friendship started innocently enough. Ruth and I had known each other slightly in college, later had been involved in youth work and counseling together, and had grown to like each other very much. Then our paths had separated for a couple of years, and when we became acquainted again—both of us away from home by then—I was dismayed to find that she had lost out spiritually. Although a professing Christian, even a graduate of an outstanding Christian college, Ruth had become cynical and bitter, full of intellectual doubts. I was desperately concerned about her during a visit she made to see me, and after a few days together, as I talked and prayed with her, I had the joy of seeing her renew her relationship with the Lord.

As events unfolded, we were soon working in the same organization and living in the same building. Naturally, we were together a great deal. She continued to be a weak Christian— occasionally giving way to former habits, easily discouraged and disillusioned, moody, and filled with doubts. She felt the need of someone to be a kind of spiritual prop for her, and I was only too glad to have her lean on me.

Meanwhile, I was becoming more and more emotionally involved. When Ruth was in a happy frame of mind emotionally and spiritually, I was happy. When she was blue and depressed, I was blue and depressed. This affected me to the point of nausea many times. I had moments of uneasiness about our relationship, but I tried to explain them away on the grounds that Ruth and I had achieved one of those rare "David–Jonathan" friendships, and that we were merely fulfilling the scriptural command to "love one another fervently."

After all, I thought I knew something about homosexuality. I thought that kind of thing was practiced only by "queer" people and neither of us was queer. At one time I had been employed in the law-enforcement agency of a large city and had direct knowledge of some of the perversions that came to the attention of its officers. These cases involved only odd, maladjusted individuals and not anyone I would know—and certainly not a Christian, I reasoned.

But one night Ruth, in one of her fed-up-with-being-a-Christian moods, began making overtures that I at last recognized for what they were. She didn't know why I would not give her the loving she needed! She flung herself across the bed where I had been reading and began to plead with me. Thoroughly frightened, I pointed out that it would be wrong in God's sight for me to yield to her demands. Besides, I couldn't hope to satisfy her. I still shiver when I recall that interlude. She could easily have overpowered me if she'd tried since she was stronger than I, and moreover had had the advantage of a course in judo.

I continued to insist quietly that I could not do what she wanted. Never in my life have I been more conscious of the mighty power of Satan who was controlling her, nor of the even mightier power of the Holy Spirit Who controlled me and was enabling me to resist her. In a few moments, she gave up the effort and never again attempted it. I had put to test the Scripture, "Resist the devil, and he will flee from you," and found it true.[1]

Susan goes on to talk about the change in relationship with Ruth and how they very shortly lost contact. She admits to still feeling enormous fear at the

[1]"Love Affair—Wrong Kind," *HIS* (March 1966): 5–6. Reprinted by permission from HIS, student magazine of Inter-Varsity Christian Fellowship, © 1966.

memory of the occasion, thinking how close she had come to being involved in a behavior she would never have thought possible and that surely would have only encouraged Ruth to stumble more deeply into the dark quagmire of her homosexuality. Susan talks about fourteen pairs of young women she knows personally who have been caught up in similar relationships and indicates that two thirds were in Christian service at the time of their involvement! Although overt homosexual practices were not present in every case, there was that constant presence of danger from which even the strongest Christian may not be exempt.

The lesson is surely clear. Love, acceptance, and counseling of a homosexual is a risk. The Christian who is led of God to take this risk must beware of becoming too caught up in the emotional and spiritual problems of his or her friend. The words of Galatians 6:1 ring true even to the present hour: "Brothers, if a man is trapped in some sin, you who are spiritual should restore him gently. But watch yourself; you also may be tempted" (NIV).

APPENDIX 4

A CASE STUDY IN HOMOSEXUAL REGENERATION

The following is an interview between the author and a young man who has been rescued by God from a tragic involvement with homosexuality. The name listed for the person interviewed is fictitious.

Dr. G: Greg, how did you happen to become an inmate here at Apalachee?

Greg: I am presently serving a ten-year sentence at Apalachee Correctional Institute (ACI) for two counts of lewd and lascivious assault upon a child under the age of fourteen years. I have been incarcerated now for over ten months and have been here at ACI almost that full time.

Dr. G: The charge sounds like the kind of thing we might expect from some inner-city ghetto experience; what is your educational and family background?

Greg: I am the youngest of three children. I have a brother who is ten years older than I, and a sister who is eight years older. I am currently thirty-two years old. Born in Patuxent, Maryland, my family moved to Florida when I was eight years old. My father was college educated as are my sister and brother. I graduated from high school and then spent four years in the Army, stationed in the Far East, Massachusetts, and Miami, Florida.

Following discharge from the Army in 1967, I returned to Tampa to attend the University of South Florida. I graduated in 1972 with a Bachelor's degree in American studies, which is a sort of generic major in American history, philosophy, humanities, political science, economics, and other disciplines. My first position was with the Boy Scouts of America as an assistant district scout executive.

Dr. G: After the scouting experience, what kind of employment situation did your education lead to in the early years of your career?

Greg: I enrolled at the Florida State University College of Law in September, 1972, and received my Juris-Doctor degree in law and began practicing law in January, 1975. In May of 1975, I was admitted to the Florida Bar and engaged in private practice until October, 1975, when I worked full time with the state attorney's office for the Second Judicial Circuit. From January until October, I had been a half-time state attorney for the juvenile division. It was my responsibility to prosecute cases involving acts of juvenile delinquency, dependency, and what was known then as children in need of supervision, such as run-away cases, ungovernable behaviors, and so forth. When I went full time with the state attorney, I was then transferred to the felony trial division and became a senior trial assistant.

Dr. G: Greg, you've said nothing about women during these busy years of career concentration. Did you have any marriage relationships during this time?

Greg: In 1970 I was married to a registered nurse, but the marriage ended in divorce in July of 1974. I subsequently married again in January, 1977, but that second marriage terminated in divorce three weeks later when the morals indictment hit.

Dr. G: In our confused society, two marriages and two divorces in seven years is not terribly unusual, but since we know that homosexuality played a role in your marital problems, I'm led to ask whether you can look back on any experiences or events of your earlier life which may have made you a "poor risk" for marriage?

Greg: Well, my childhood was not particularly happy as the youngest of three children. I was very over-valued, over-protected, and spoiled. At the same time, there was an underlying tone of ambivalence and hostility on the part of my parents which may largely be attributed to the fact that my parents had lost a daughter when she was nine years old (some six or seven years before my birth) and I think the latent feelings against my older sister who had passed away were directed in part against me. This attitude was very subtle, however, and I don't think they were even aware of it at any time.

Dr. G: What about religion? My research indicates that many homosexuals were very religious, even fundamentalistic about their religious beliefs during childhood and teen years. Did you come out of a background like that?

Greg: I was not raised in a Christian home. My parents were members of a church and attended regularly, both active in the choir, but from my present perspective, I can realize now that they were not born again. I resented church from a very early age, feeling it was meaningless. At about thirteen years of age I terminated all my relationships with the church and quit attending. After entering the Army I received instruction from the Roman Catholic church and was eventually baptized and confirmed in that faith. I remained an active Roman Catholic for a period of about a year and a half, but then my participation dwindled to nothing. Again, my religious experience still had nothing to do with Jesus Christ.

Dr. G: When and how did your homosexual involvement with boys begin?

Greg: The activity at first was innocuous. I had tremendous peer group relationship problems after coming to a new community where I was kind of a bookish, Yankee kid who didn't appreciate things like sports and fishing. I was desperate for acceptance at that age (eight or nine) and homosexuality brought the first acceptance I had received from my peer group since we moved to Florida. The activity continued in varying degrees throughout elementary school and into junior high school.

There was another thing. In eighth grade I was beginning to get interested in girls, as kids usually do at that age. But I had a very bitter experience with a young girl with whom I was very much enamored. I had asked her for a date, she accepted, and then stood me up. I remember several instances like that. A contemporaneously bad experience was one of my homosexual incidents becoming public knowledge in the junior high school. I was humiliated by my peer group and subsequently suppressed any public involvement.

Later my sexual contacts increased with people who were younger than I. The homosexual activities continued again with varying degrees of frequency. There were periods of time up to a year in which I had absolutely no contact and then there were other periods in which contacts were very frequent. These continued from that point until my arrest in 1977. It is interesting to note that the homosexual experiences did not occur with kids who were strangers, that is there were never any kind of street corner pick-up situations. I'm not justifying private homosexual activity but just describing my actions. These kids were always very close to me and I was usually close to their families.

Dr. G: It seems obvious, Greg, that like many homosexuals, you were actually bisexual, maintaining a relationship with your wife while at the same time having some occasional relationships with young boys. How did the divorce in 1974 affect your homosexual propensity and practice?

Greg: In July, 1974, matters continued to really deteriorate with regard to my sexual behavior. The number and frequency of instances increased, and as the Scripture points out, I became more and more abandoned to sin. About the same time I got divorced, I began living with a family. When I was having a lot of financial difficulties, the boy and I became sexually involved. And although the sexual part of the relationship was very strong for a period of time during the almost three years the relationship lasted, the sexual relationship didn't dominate our lives. But I became so attached to this particular boy that he became an alter ego. I was incapable of functioning and didn't go any place he didn't go, becoming very anxious and terribly insecure if I was away from him for any period of time. In any event, my second wife and I eventually got involved in litigation with the boy's mother over his custody. That broke the story in public with all its legal implications. That occurred in January, 1977.

Dr. G: I understand, Greg, that you're currently engaged to be married a third time. Can you tell us a little bit about this relationship?

Greg: She's a Christian and has come through some

difficult experiences. Donna has been very sensitive to my situation. Not only is she a Christian, but she's a social worker who has had extensive experience in dealing with people and problems. She is a candidate for a Master's degree in criminal justice.

Donna and I became very closely involved and after a certain period of time it was clear that we were falling very much in love. I think our initial feeling for each other, certainly in my case, was one of just outright desperation. During the period of time that I have been incarcerated though, Donna and I have watched our relationship grow very strong in a Christ-based relationship. For the first time in my life, in prison with a ten-year sentence, I am having a healthy, mature, responsible relationship with a female!

Dr. G: There seems to be a warmth, almost a happiness, in your attitude toward Donna and the expectation of this normal relationship. Yet we are told again and again that homosexuals can find this kind of normal happy relationship with other persons of the same sex—presumably the concept "gay" carries at least some of that idea of being at peace with one's homosexuality. How do you respond to that?

Greg: First of all, I think that the term "gay" is such a grossly abused term with regard to homosexuals. I have seen some homosexuals that psychiatric or psychological professionals refer to as well-adjusted. But I am convinced, based on numerous conversations and observations of people whom I've known both in prison and out who have a homosexual preference, that there is no such thing as a happy homosexual; they are *anything but* gay.

Secondly, I believe there are no sociological arguments that can be made against homosexuality except that it does not reproduce the race. It is a useless kind of argument to suggest that homosexuality is intrinsically wrong *based on society's quicksand kind of sexual morality*. The single factor that makes homosexuality genuinely, morally wrong is Scripture. But I do believe that society's fear of them is well taken. Perhaps the fear itself is conviction from the Holy Spirit in a society in which man is separated from God.

Dr. G: Greg, you have had a unique look at homosexuality from the viewpoint of a practitioner, a social worker, an attorney, and now inside prison walls as a convict. Varying views in our culture identify homosexuality as sin, sickness, and of course more recently, as an alternative sexual life-style. From your close-up perspective how would you describe it?

Greg: The American Psychiatric Association says that homosexuality is not a disease and I don't think it is either. It is a sin. A particular kind of sin that's caused by a number of different factors. A sin like drug addiction and other kinds of sexual abuse, alcoholism, and so on that we see rampant in our society.

Psychiatrists and psychologists have had a noticeable failure rate with homosexuality in the same sense they have had with drug addiction and alcoholism. I think it is largely because they do not understand the problem. I am of the opinion that what is fundamentally wrong with homosexuals is a spiritual malady and not a physical, intellectual, or moral one. And as long as we continue to fish around in the cesspool of humanistic psychology to try to find the answers, the problems like homosexuality will continue to multiply.

It is an absolute to me that the healing power of Jesus Christ can solve any kind of problem in any man's life. I don't really care what kind of problem it is. Homosexuality, like chewing one's fingernails, or drinking, or being a procrastinator with regard to your Christian duties and so forth are just all alike. They are sin. They are separation from God. The same healing strength of Christ can be present in the life of the homosexual just as easily as it is in the life of a drug addict, an alcoholic, or any other form of spiritual deviate.

Dr. G: You've used the word "cure" several times and have identified homosexuality, in your opinion, as essentially a spiritual problem. Is the cure then also essentially a spiritual cure?

Greg: I am of the opinion that Christ is healing me. I am committed to the idea that He is going to make me an effective tool for His will. I have yielded my life to Christ as completely as I can. I still have a long way to go and I suspect that we all do, but I pray every day that Christ will take my life and will use it for His witness, and to reach other people with this tremendous message.

Dr. G: I notice, Greg, that you are using present tense verbs indicating that the "cure" was not necessarily instantaneous but as in some of the other problems you mentioned, such as drug addiction or alcoholism, God may be working in the new believer's life for some time to bring about a complete healing. Am I understanding you correctly on that?

Greg: Yes. I believe that the Lord is going to cure me. I claim that promise. I know that as long as I am in fellowship with God and other Christians; as long as I stay in the Word; as long as I continue to grow in Christ; as long as I lead a Christ-honoring life; as long as my relationship with my future wife is Christ-based, the Lord can use me.

Dr. G: What about the shame, the guilt which has been associated with your homosexual past? Certainly, the public exposure of this whole mess has been enormously traumatic. Is the power of Christ sufficient to deal with that as well?

Greg: I am not proud, obviously, of the life I have lived, or the things that brought me here. I am beginning in some very important ways to lose my shame of it. That is, I have lost the guilt through the forgiveness of Christ and I don't want to advertise my background so as to maybe be a stumbling block to others or damage my witness. But I no longer quake in fear of the notion of leaving the institutional setting and turning to freedom in a physical sense and conducting my life. I don't ever want to live my life in darkness again. Donna and I have committed ourselves to the whole concept of 1 John that we want to live our lives "in the light." We want to be effective for the Lord in whatever way He sees fit to use us.

Dr. G: Thank you, Greg, for sharing this very intimate picture of your life with thousands of readers. I am willing to predict that this testimony will not only be used of God to help many people struggling with the homosexual problem, but will also influence great numbers of dedicated Christians to pray for you and Donna as you seek God's will in putting your life back together and using it to serve Christ.

Greg: As the days go on, I hope that you're successful in this effort; that somehow the Word of Christ can reach out to the people who are in similar situations to those I was in. The most awful feeling in the world is the emptiness that people inevitably have under those circumstances. It is important to stress the *grace* of the gospel because when you're living that kind of a life it's hard to believe you are good enough to become a Christian. The whole message of salvation was never communicated to me on a level that I could or was willing to understand. The church needs to understand this problem and to pay very close attention to the patience and love which needs to be shown to homosexuals if they're going to be brought to the Lord. They seem so desperate and when we can get past the fear, the hostility, the avoidance techniques that every homosexual uses, then the message of Christ can become clear. There is real hope.

SCRIPTURE REFERENCE INDEX

BIBLIOGRAPHY

Books

Allen C. "The Letter to the Romans." In *A New Testament Commentary*. G.C.D. Howley, ed. Grand Rapids: Zondervan, 1969.

Arndt, William F. and Gingrich, Wilbur. *A Greek-English Lexicon of the New Testament and Other Early Christian Literature,* Fourth Revised Edition, S.V. Chicago: Univ. of Chicago Press, 1957.

Bailey, D. Sherwin. *Homosexuality and the Western Christian Tradition*. New York: Longmans, 1955. Reprinted in Hamden, Conn: Archon, 1975.

Barnhouse, Donald Gray. *Genesis, A Devotional Commentary*. Grand Rapids: Zondervan, 1970.

Benson, Rod. *In Defense of Homosexuality*. New York: Julian Press, 1965.

Cole, William. *Sex and Love in the Bible*. New York: Association Press, 1959.

Davidson, Alex. *The Returns of Love*. Downers Grove, Illinois: InterVarsity Press, 1970.

Drakeford, John. *Forbidden Love*. Waco, Texas: Word Books, 1971.

Ellicott, Charles John. *A Bible Commentary For English Readers,* vol. 2. London: Cassell and Company, Ltd., n.d.

Ellis, Albert. *Homosexuality: Its Causes and Cure*. New York: Lyle Stewart Inc., 1965.

Gaebelein, Frank E., ed. *Expositor's Bible Commentary*. Grand Rapids: Zondervan, 1976.

Jones, Clinton R. *Homosexuality and Counseling*. Philadelphia: Fortress Press, 1974.

Keil, C. F. and F. Delitzsch. *Biblical Commentary on the Old Testament*. "Joshua, Judges, Ruth." Grand Rapids: Eerdmans, reprinted 1950.

Kelso, James A. *Archaeology and the Ancient Testament*. Grand Rapids: Zondervan, 1968.

Kidner, Derek, *Genesis*. Downers Grove, Ill.: InterVarsity Press, 1967.

Kraeling, Emil G. *Bible Atlas*. Chicago: Rand McNally and Company, 1956.

Leupold, H. C. *Exposition of Genesis*. Columbus, Ohio: The Wartburg Press, 1967.

Lewis, C. S. *The Four Loves*. London: Fontana Books, 1960.

Neufeld, E. *Ancient Hebrew Marriage Laws*. London: Green and Company, 1944.

Nicoll, W. Robertson, ed. *The Expositor's Bible*, vol. VII, Robert A. Watson, "Judges and Ruth." London: Hodder and Stoughton, 1889.

Pfeiffer Charles F. and Harrison Everett F., eds. *The Wycliffe Bible Commentary*. Chicago: Moody Press, 1962.

Rodgers, William D. *The Gay Invasion*. Denver: Accent Books, 1977.

Scanzoni, Letha and Mollenkott, Virginia. *Is the Homosexual My Neighbor? Another Christian View* New York: Harper & Row, 1978.

Schultz, Samuel J. *The Old Testament Speaks*. New York: Harper & Row, 1960.

Situation Ethics: A Dialogue Between Joseph Fletcher and John Montgomery. Minneapolis: Dimension Books, 1972.

Stiflar, James. *The Epistle to the Romans*. Chicago: Moody Press, 1974.

Thielicke, Helmut, *The Ethics of Sex*. New York: Harper and Row, 1964.

Unger, Merrill F. *Archaeology and the Old Testament*. Grand Rapids: Zondervan, 1954.

Unger, Merrill F. *Unger's Bible Dictionary*. Chicago: Moody Press, 1957.

Watts, J. W. *A Distinctive Translation of Genesis*. Grand Rapids: Eerdmans, 1963.

West, Morris. *The Devil's Advocate*. New York: William Morrow, Inc., 1959.

White, John. *Eros Defiled*. Downers Grove, Illinois: InterVarsity Press, 1977.

Periodicals, Monographs, and Other Materials

Adams, Jay E. "Resolving Sexual Difficulties." Originally published in *The Christian Counselor's Manual* (Philadelphia: Presbyterian and Reformed Publishing Co., 1973). Quoted by Howard A. Eyrich in *The Journal of Pastoral Practice*, vol. 1, no. 2 (Summer 1977).

"Are Homosexuals Necessary?" American Institute of Family Relations, no. 542.

Bevis, Jim. "How One Church Handles Homosexuals." *Christian Life*, November 1977, pp. 24–25, 58.

"The Bible and the Homosexual." *Christianity Today*, 19 January 1968, p. 25.

Blair, Ralph. "An Evangelical Look at Homosexuality." Originally published as "The Gay Evangelical." In *Homosexuality and Religion*, number 13 in the Monograph Series of the National Task Force on Student Personnel Service and Homosexuality, 1972.

Bockmühl, Klaus. "Homosexuality and Biblical Perspective. *Christianity Today*, 16 February 1973, p. 14.

Chance, Paul and Hooker, Evelyn. "Facts that Liberated the Gay Community." *Psychology Today*, December 1975 p. 12.

"Charting the Gay Life." *Newsweek*, 27 March 1978, pp. 98 100.

Cowles, Robert. "Gay as in Gomorrah." *The Christian Reader*, November-December 1977, p. 16.

Custance, Arthur C. "Some Remarkable Biblical Confirmations from Archaeology with Special Emphasis on the Book of Genesis." Dorway Paper no. 39. Ottawa, Canada, 1963

DeLong, Burl A. "A Critique of Current Evangelical Interpretation Regarding the Biblical Understanding of Homosexuality." Master's Degree Thesis, Dallas Theological Seminary, May 1977.

"Diagnostic and Statistical Manual of Mental Health." American Psychiatric Association, 2nd ed., Washington D. C., 1975.

Dolby, James R. "Helping the Homosexual." *Christianity Today*, 16 February 1968, pp. 29–30.

"Door Interview: Anita Bryant." *Wittenburg Door*, no. 39 October-November 1977, p. 13.

Driver, Tom F. "Love Needs Law." *Religion and Life*, Spring 1966, p. 200.

"An Evangelical Look at Homosexuality." New York: Homosexual Community Counseling Center, 1972.

Evans, G. Russell. "What about the Homosexual?" *The Presbyterian Journal*, 30 November 1977, pp. 7–8.

Eyrich, Howard. "Hope for the Homosexual." *The Journal of Pastoral Practice*, November 1977.

"Gays and the Law." *Newsweek*, 25 October 1976, p. 103.

"Gays on the March." *Time*, 8 September 1975, p. 32.

"An Historic Dialogue . . . Homosexuality: A Gift From God?" *Inspiration*, March/April 1978.

Hoffman, Martin. "Homosexuality." *Today's Education NEA Journal*, November 1970, p. 21.

'Homosexuality, Parts I–IV." *Christian Life*, August-November 1977.

The Homosexual: Newly Visible, Newly Understood." *Time*, 31 October 1969, p. 61.

'Homosexual Ordination: Bishops Feel the Flack." *Christianity Today*, 4 March 1977, p. 51.

Johnson, Lewis S., Jr. "God Gave Them Up." *Bibliotheca Sacra*, April-June 1972, pp. 127–29.

Kirk, Jerry R. "Consultation on Homosexuality." Unpublished monograph, College Hill Presbyterian Church, Cincinnati, Ohio, n.d.

Landis, Clarence W. "Homosexuality from a Biblical Perspective." *Trinity Journal*, vol. 6, no. 1, Spring 1977.

Landis, Judson T. "Experiences of 500 Children with Adult Sexual Deviations." In *Psychiatric Quarterly Supplement*, State Hospital's Press, New York, 1956.

'Letter from a Homosexual." *Christianity Today*, 1 March 1968, p. 23.

Lindsell, Harold. "Homosexuals and the Church." *Christianity Today*, 28 September 1973, p. 12.

"Love Affair—Wrong Kind." *HIS*, March 1966, pp. 5–6.

Lovelace, Richard. "How Evangelicals Should Respond to the Homosexual Issue." *Evangelical Newsletter*, vol. 4, no. 9, 23 September 1977, p. 4.

"The Militant Homosexual." *Newsweek*, 23 August 1971, p. 48.

Mullen, Stanley H. "The Homosexual, Does He Belong in the Church?" *Christian Life*, October 1967, p. 39.

O'Leary, Jean and Vida, Ginny. "Lesbians and the Schools." Homosexual Community Counseling Center, 921 Madison Avenue, New York.

Perry, Troy. "Homosexual Ordination: Bishops Feel the Flack." *Christianity Today,* 4 March 1977, p. 51.

Peterson, William J. "The Evangelical Mood at the End of 1977." *Evangelical Newsletter,* vol. 4, no. 24, 2 December 1977, p. 4.

"Policing the Third Sex." *Newsweek,* 27 October 1969, p. 76.

Popenoe, Paul. "Are Homosexuals Necessary?" American Institute of Family Relations, no. 542.

Roth, Wolfgang. "What of Sodom and Gomorrah?" *Explor 1,* Fall 1975, p. 10.

"San Francisco Gays Gaining Political Clout." *Fort Lauderdale News,* 4 December 1977, p. 18C.

Scanzoni, Letha. "On Friendship and Homosexuality." *Christianity Today,* 27 September 1974, p. 10.

Sims, Bennett J. "Sex and Homosexuality." *Christianity Today,* 24 February 1978, pp. 23–30.

Smedes, Lewis B. "Homosexuality: Sorting out the Issues. ' *The Reformed Journal,* January 1978.

Stablinski, Kim. "Homosexuality, What the Bible Does and Does Not Say." *The Ladder,* July 1969.

Tibe, Raymond L. "A Critical Evaluation of the Rationale Used in Support of Male Homosexuality Among Christians." Master's Degree thesis, Trinity Evangelical Divinity School, 1973.

Trends (Program Agency of the United Presbyterian Church), July/August 1973, p. 6.

"United Presbyterians: Bracing for Battle." *Christianity Today,* 10 February 1978, p. 48.

"U. S. Catholic Bishops Revise Guides on Teaching of Faith. ' *The Miami Herald,* 18 November 1977, p. 28A.

Young, Charles. "Homosexuality and the Campus." *HIS,* February 1966, p. 14.